W9-AEO-855

"AMERICAN SOCIETY FOR QUALITY -
QIC"

ISO 9001 REQUIREMENTS

92 REQUIREMENTS CHECKLIST AND COMPLIANCE GUIDE

Fourth Edition

JACK KANHOLM

AQA Co. ▪ Los Angeles

© 2002 by AQA Co.

ISBN   1-882711-25-4

AQA Co.
155 S. El Molino Ave.
Pasadena, CA 91101
Phn: (626) 796 9000
Fax: (626) 796 9070

Printed in the United States of America

PREFACE

The new ISO 9000:2000 family of standards consists of the following three standards:

- ISO 9000:2000 Quality Management Systems — Fundamentals and Vocabulary;
- ISO 9001:2000 Quality Management Systems — Requirements; and
- ISO 9004:2000 Quality Management Systems — Guidelines for Performance Improvement.

For the purpose of ISO 9000 certification audits, only ISO 9001 specifies mandatory requirements.

Note that the old ISO 9002 and ISO 9003 standards are discontinued. Organizations that do not design or develop products and/or services and thus were certified to ISO 9002 will now have to use ISO 9001, but can exclude design and development requirements from the scope. Specific rules for excluding inapplicable requirements are stipulated in the standard in Clause 1.2, Application.

This book identifies and explains 92 distinct requirements of ISO 9001:2000, Clauses 4 through 8. These clauses provide the specification for the certification audit of quality management systems. The requirements are interpreted and explained from a point of view of a certification audit.

The purpose of this book is to identify all auditable requirements and explain how these requirements should be satisfied on the level of documentation, implementation, and records; and to offer some insight on how auditors will verify compliance with each requirement. The unique aspect of this book is the systematic and disciplined approach to the identification of all auditable requirements, and reinterpretation of these requirements into a definitive action list that must be implemented to achieve full conformance. This first step of precisely identifying the requirements and interpreting them correctly is the most difficult one for most organizations. Once this step is taken, the project of implementing ISO 9000 can be properly planned and carried out with full confidence that the effort will result in successful certification.

This book is intended for managers and teams charged with the responsibility of implementing ISO 9000 quality management system in their organizations and getting the system certified. While the book is written specifically for this group, anyone interested in a detailed and comprehensive interpretation of ISO 9000 should find it useful and interesting. The book can be successfully used for training auditors, and will provide valuable reference for registrars and consultants.

This book is the leading title in the AQA ISO 9000 series. The other two publications are *ISO 9000 Documentation* (software) and *ISO 9000 In Our Company*. The role of this book in the series is to introduce the ISO 9001 requirements and explain what needs to be done to comply. *ISO 9000 Documentation* is a software package with templates for generic quality manual and procedures, and *ISO 9000 In Our Company* is a self-study workbook for employee training. All AQA publications are annotated on the last four pages of this book and on our Internet site at **www.aqapress.com**.

The author welcomes any comments regarding his interpretation of the new requirements. Please e-mail your comments to *jack@aqapress.com* or call (626) 796-9000.

GOOD LUCK WITH YOUR ISO 9000 IMPLEMENTATION PROJECT AND CERTIFICATION OF YOUR QUALITY SYSTEM !

Jack Kanholm

The commercial viability of publishing and distributing this book depends on the copyright protection. Please note that the list of requirements in the first section of the book is also protected. If you need additional copies, please use the order form enclosed at the back of the book, or call the publisher. For any questions regarding copyright please call AQA Press at (626) 796-9000.

REQUIREMENTS

1.　SCOPE

1.1　GENERAL

No auditable requirements

1.2　APPLICATION

No auditable requirements

2.　NORMATIVE REFERENCE

No auditable requirements

3.　TERMS AND DEFINITIONS

No auditable requirements

4.　QUALITY MANAGEMENT SYSTEM

4.1　GENERAL REQUIREMENTS

4.2　DOCUMENTATION REQUIREMENTS

4.2.1　General

5.6 MANAGEMENT REVIEW

5.6.1 General

5.6.2 Review Input

5.6.3 Review Output

6 RESOURCE MANAGEMENT

6.1 PROVISION OF RESOURCES

6.2 HUMAN RESOURCES

6.2.1 General

Requirements included in 6.2.2.

6.2.2 Competence, Awareness and Training

7.3   DESIGN AND DEVELOPMENT

7.3.1   Design and Development Planning

7.3.2   Design and Development Inputs

7.3.3   Design and Development Outputs

7.3.4   Design and Development Review

7.3.5   Design and Development Verification

7.3.6   Design and Development Validation

7.3.7   Control of Design and Development Changes

7.4   PURCHASING

7.4.1   Purchasing Process

7.4.2　Purchasing Information

7.4.3　Verification of Purchased Product

7.5　PRODUCTION AND SERVICE PROVISION

7.5.1　Control of Production and Service Provision

7.5.2　Validation of Processes for Production and Service

7.5.3　Identification and Traceability

7.5.4　Customer Property

7.5.5　Preservation of Product

7.6   CONTROL OF MONITORING AND MEASURING DEVICES

8   MEASUREMENT, ANALYSIS AND IMPROVEMENT

8.1   GENERAL

8.2   MONITORING AND MEASUREMENT

8.2.1   Customer Satisfaction

8.2.2   Internal Audit

8.2.3 Monitoring and Measurement of Processes

8.2.4 Monitoring and Measurement of Product

8.3 CONTROL OF NONCONFORMING PRODUCT

8.4 ANALYSIS OF DATA

8.5 IMPROVEMENT

8.5.1 Continual Improvement

8.5.2   Corrective Action

- Investigate causes of nonconformities, take corrective actions to prevent recurrence, and review the effectiveness of actions taken. 147

8.5.3   Preventive Action

- Identify potential nonconformities and their causes and take actions to prevent their occurrence. 149

1-3 GENERAL CLAUSES

The first three introductory clauses do not contain any requirements, but are important for proper interpretation of the standard. Especially important are the definitions of the term *product* in Clauses 1.1 and 1.2.

1. SCOPE

1.1 General

This clause best demonstrates how the focus and approach have changed in the new 2000 edition of ISO 9001. In the previous edition, the purpose of the quality system was defined to be mainly the prevention of nonconformity. The new standard offers itself to organizations that want to demonstrate their ability to provide products that meet requirements, and to enhance customer satisfaction through continual improvement and prevention of nonconformity. The new key words are *customer satisfaction* and *continual improvement*.

The NOTE at the end of this clause defines the term *product* to be only the product intended for, or required by, the customer. In addition, the last sentence in Clause 3 states that the term *product* can also mean *service*. These definitions are very important as they determine which products, processes, and activities must comply with the requirements of the standard.

1.2 Application

This clause defines the rules for claiming exclusions from ISO 9001 requirements. Under previous editions of the standard, companies could choose between ISO 9001, 9002, or 9003, depending on the nature of their operations. Now there is only one specification of requirements, ISO 9001, but organizations may claim exclusions from various requirements that do not apply to their operations. The intent is to retain the flexibility of the previous configuration with only one specification.

In a nutshell, the rules are that exclusions must be limited to those within Clause 7, Product Realization, and that exclusions shall not affect the organization's ability to provide product that meets customer and regulatory requirements. There is also a warning that when permissible exclusions are exceeded, conformity to the standard may not be claimed.

The intention is primarily to allow exclusion of design control requirements where there are no design activities. Other typical applications, especially in service industries, would be exclusion of requirements related to product identification and traceability, customer property, preservation of product, and control of measuring devices.

2. NORMATIVE REFERENCES

The only interesting thing in this clause is that ISO 9004 is not mentioned as normative reference. The new ISO 9004 is no longer a guide for implementing ISO 9001, but is a guide for improving the quality system beyond ISO 9001. Thus ISO 9004 should no longer be used for interpretation of ISO 9001 requirements.

3. TERMS AND DEFINITIONS

This clause explains the new terms used for the supply chain, and the term *product*. For other definitions it refers to ISO 9000:2000.

The company implementing the standard is now referred to as *organization* (used to be *supplier*) and its subcontractors are referred to as *suppliers*.

Product is defined to also mean *service*.

The whole vocabulary of ISO 9000:2000 sounds different. System elements are called *processes*; inspections and testing are called *product verification* and *validation*; production is called *realization*; and so forth. These changes were intended to take out the vocabulary that identified the standard with manufacturing. The idea was to make the standard more appealing to service industries.

QUALITY MANAGEMENT SYSTEM

4.1   GENERAL REQUIREMENTS

REQUIREMENT   *Establish, document, implement, and maintain a quality management system, and continually improve its effectiveness.*

IMPLEMENTATION   Requirements in this clause, including the list (a) through (f), are very broad and general, and are not unique. All will be repeated later in other clauses of the standard. Thus, this clause will be satisfied automatically when the whole standard is implemented. The only thing that needs to be done at this point is to acknowledge this clause with a corresponding policy statement in the quality manual.

Note how the word *process* is used in this clause, and throughout the standard. In the 2000 edition of ISO 9001, the quality system consists of interrelated processes, with outputs from one process being used as inputs in subsequent processes. Consequently, what used to be called quality system *element* or *activity* is now referred to as *process*.

Strictly speaking, a quality system process, as defined in ISO 9000, is not the same as a quality system element. But for people used to the old terminology, especially in manufacturing where the word *process* is reserved to mean production process, the new vocabulary may be somewhat confusing.

Using the old terminology and simplifying the language, the list of actions required in this clause would read as follows:

a) Identify elements required for your system;

b) Determine sequence and interaction of the elements;

c) Design each element, i.e., determine what, who and when; what are the inputs and outputs; how documented; what records to maintain; etc.

d) Ensure that each element is sufficiently documented (procedures, work instructions, etc.) and that the required input data and information are communicated;

e) Check and analyze the implementation of each element (internal audits and quality performance data);

f) Implement corrective and preventive actions, and continually improve effectiveness of the system.

DOCUMENTATION To acknowledge this general requirement, the quality manual should include commitments to establish, document, implement, maintain, and improve the quality system. This would usually appear in one of the introductory sections of the manual, or in the sections dealing with management commitment.

RECORDS All records and the entire documentation are relevant for demonstrating compliance with this requirement. Especially important are internal audit reports and corrective and preventive action records, and the evidence that the quality system is being continually improved.

AUDIT Auditors would raise a finding against this clause only when there is a fundamental and general problem with the quality system. For example, when the quality system is not fully implemented or is not being maintained.

REQUIREMENT *Ensure control over those outsourced processes that may affect product conformity.*

IMPLEMENTATION The last paragraph of Clause 4.1 requires that the quality system be extended to also control outsourced (subcontracted) processes, especially those that may affect product conformity. The nature and degree of these controls are not specified. Thus, anything that is being done to prevent nonconformities in purchased or subcontracted products or services can be credited as a response to this requirement.

In cases where purchasing and subcontracting is limited to procurement of materials or individual components, this general requirement can be satisfied automatically by implementing Clause 7.4, Purchasing. This would provide such basic controls as supplier evaluation and monitoring, and verification of purchased product (receiving inspection). However, if subcontractors perform complete product design, are responsible for most of product realization, or are otherwise providing significant operational capability, much more will be expected. In these cases, some elements of the quality system must be actually extended to directly control subcontracted processes, or the subcontractor's quality system must be capable of and be trusted to provide the required control.

DOCUMENTATION At this stage, it is sufficient to acknowledge this general requirement by a corresponding commitment in the quality manual. Specific methods for ensuring proper control of subcontracted processes would normally be developed under clauses dealing with purchasing (7.4) and verification of purchased product (7.4.3).

RECORDS The evidence of compliance will consist of documentation defining how subcontracted processes are controlled and records demonstrating implementation. The documents may be purchase orders, contracts, specifications, procedures, instructions, etc. The records could be subcontractor audit reports, process SPC records, product inspection records, or anything else that would demonstrate that the specified controls have been fully implemented.

AUDIT Auditors will write a finding against this clause only when the control of subcontracted processes is not addressed in the quality system, or there is a total breakdown of these controls. Otherwise, more specific problems related to the control of subcontractors and purchased products will fall under clauses dealing with purchasing (7.4) and verification of purchased product (7.4.3). A typical nonconformity in this category would be a failure to communicate or enforce flow-down requirements.

4.2   DOCUMENTATION REQUIREMENTS

4.2.1   General

REQUIREMENT   *Document the quality system, including written statements of quality policy and objectives, quality manual, procedures, and records.*

IMPLEMENTATION   This clause defines the required scope for the quality system documentation.

Item (a) requires documented quality policy and objectives. Quality policy is usually documented in the quality manual. Quality objectives for products are often documented in technical specifications and drawings; objectives for the quality system are usually documented in management review reports. More detailed discussion of the policy and objectives will follow under Clauses 5.3 and 5.4.1.

Item (b) requires a quality manual. The scope and format of the quality manual will be discussed in detail under Clause 4.2.2, Quality Manual.

Item (c) requires documented procedures. ISO 9001 explicitly mentions documented procedures in only six instances: for document control, control of records, internal audits, control of nonconforming product, corrective action, and preventive action. However, in practice, an average quality system would have many more procedures, as needed to ensure its effective operation (refer to the next requirement).

Item (d) requires any additional documentation necessary to ensure effective operation and control (mostly additional procedures and work instructions). This is discussed further under the next requirement.

Finally, item (e) requires records providing evidence of product conformity and of the effective operation of the quality system. Records will be further discussed under Clause 4.2.4.

DOCUMENTATION The general scope of the quality system documentation should be defined in the quality manual. In addition, the operational procedure for document control (required in Clause 4.2.3) should define the scope of its application, i.e., define the categories of documents that must be controlled.

Some companies may actually want to have a separate procedure for defining the scope and general rules for quality system documentation. Such a procedure (QOP-42-01) is included in Jack Kanholm's *ISO 9001 Documentation* software.

RECORDS The evidence of compliance is simply the existence of the required types of documents.

AUDIT Auditors will always review the quality manual and operational procedures before the audit. This is usually done a couple of weeks in advance of the audit to allow for addressing any problems that may be identified by the review. Other documents, such as quality policy, quality objectives, work instructions, and records will be examined during the audit. The adequacy of these documents, especially work instructions, can only be properly evaluated in the field, i.e., while witnessing the actual activities and operations that are defined in the documents.

REQUIREMENT *Establish additional documentation as required to ensure the effective planning, operation, and control of quality system processes (elements).*

IMPLEMENTATION As mentioned under the previous requirement, ISO 9001 explicitly requires documented procedures in only six instances: for document control, control of records, internal audits, control of nonconforming product, corrective action, and preventive action.

However, item (d) of this clause potentially broadens the requirement for documentation to include additional procedures and/or work instructions where this is needed to ensure the effective planning, operation and control of the quality system.

The criteria to determine when an additional documented procedure or work instruction is needed are not defined in the standard. Traditionally, a written instruction is expected whenever methods or rules for an activity, operation, or element (quality system process) are more complex than what an average person can memorize. Another consideration is consistency. All people who do the same thing must have the same understanding of how to carry out the activity and what the rules are. For example, all internal auditors must document their audit findings in the same way.

DOCUMENTATION

The quality manual should communicate the policy that documentation of the quality system shall be developed to the extent necessary to ensure effective and consistent operation of the system. Optionally, this could be further developed in relevant operational procedures to include specific criteria for determining the need for additional documentation. Jack Kanholm's *ISO 9001 Documentation* includes such a procedure defining the criteria for the need to establish work instructions (QOP-75-02).

RECORDS

The evidence of compliance will be provided in itself by the additional documentation.

AUDIT

To test whether the scope of the quality system documentation is sufficient, auditors will witness or review the results of those activities for which there are no written instructions. When they find mistakes, failures, or inconsistencies, they would interpret them as evidence that written documentation for these activities is insufficient.

4.2.2   Quality Manual

REQUIREMENT   *Establish a quality manual to describe the quality system, and to document or reference operational procedures.*

IMPLEMENTATION   The role of the quality manual is much more important in the new 2000 edition than in previous editions of the standard. This is because the requirements for documented procedures have been reduced dramatically. Now the quality manual is the only document that systematically defines all processes (elements) of the quality system and their mutual interrelation.

The most effective compliance strategy that would minimize unnecessary documentation is to have a fully developed quality manual systematically addressing all clauses of the standard, and just a minimum number of procedures that are either explicitly required (six instances) or are truly useful. With this approach, some sections of the manual will in fact become mini-procedures. There is no problem with this, as ISO 9001 explicitly allows procedures to be directly documented in the quality manual.

DOCUMENTATION   There is usually no need for confirming or acknowledging requirements of this clause in the quality manual or operational procedures. This would be like instructions on how to write a manual in the manual that is already written.

RECORDS   The quality manual itself will provide the evidence of its own adequacy.

AUDIT   Auditors will expect the quality manual to be complete, i.e., to address every clause and every requirement of the standard. Where a process is further documented in a procedure or work instruction, its description in the manual can be very brief, and include references to the more detailed documents. Otherwise, where the process is not documented elsewhere, the description in the manual should be sufficiently detailed to stand on its own in defining the process.

22   **ISO 9001 REQUIREMENTS**

REQUIREMENT

Identify and justify in the quality manual any exclusions of ISO 9001 requirements.

IMPLEMENTATION

This requirement relates to the new structure of the ISO 9000:2000 family of standards (ISO 9002 and ISO 9003 don't exist any more), and a general recognition that some elements of the specified quality system will not apply to all organizations.

Rules regarding exclusions are discussed under Clause 1.2, Application.

DOCUMENTATION

Exclusions of requirements and their justification may be documented in a special introductory section of the quality manual, or within the body of the manual under relevant sections where the exclusions apply.

RECORDS

Statements of exclusions and their justification are in themselves sufficient to demonstrate compliance with this requirement. To be acceptable, exclusions must conform with rules stated in Clause 1.2, Application.

AUDIT

Auditors will verify that exclusions are formally documented in the quality manual, including their justification, and that they follow the rules of Clause 1.2. Auditors will also make their own independent judgement of whether justifications for the exclusions are proper and accurate.

If a justification for an exclusion is found to be inappropriate, this will usually result in a major nonconformity. For example, when design control requirements are exempted in a company that actually designs or modifies the design of products.

4.2.3   Control of Documents

REQUIREMENT

Review and approve documents prior to issue.

IMPLEMENTATION

Every controlled document must be approved for adequacy prior to issue. The approval should be evidenced by a signature, or by other means, identifying the authorized person who approved the document. The approval signature usually distinguishes an issued document from its draft or preliminary versions. For electronic documents, issuing a document takes the form of posting the document on the network. In this case, there should be some record (e-mail or log) evidencing that documents posted on the network have been reviewed and approved. The authority to approve and issue documents must be defined for all categories of controlled documents.

DOCUMENTATION   The general document control procedure should have a section dealing specifically with the review and approval of documents. The procedure should explain the manner and scope of review, and define the level of authority required to approve and issue various types of documents.

RECORDS   Signatures on documents provide the required record and evidence of compliance. For documents in electronic media the record of approval may be separate from the document itself. This may be signatures in document release logs, or e-mails authorizing posting of particular documents on the network.

AUDIT   Compliance is checked not only in the locations where documents are issued and controlled, but everywhere else they are used and stored. When examining documents, auditors always look for review and approval status. It is a reflex.

REQUIREMENT   *Update documents and reapprove changes and revisions of documents.*

IMPLEMENTATION   Approval of revisions involving reissue of a document on a higher revision level would usually follow the same procedure that applies to issuing of initial documents.

Handwritten corrections in documents, often called red-line corrections, must also be reviewed and approved. Anything crossed out, added, or changed in a controlled document must be signed by an authorized person. Red-line corrections should not be left on documents indefinitely. Documents should be reissued after a practical number of changes have been made.

Handwritten notes and comments on documents should be avoided. Even though the notes do not modify the original content of a document, they add new information that is not authorized and will be lost when the document is reissued and the marked-up copy destroyed.

DOCUMENTATION   The operational procedure dealing with document changes should instruct how to request changes in documents; provide rules for making corrections in documents, including their review and approval; and instruct how documents should be reissued on a higher revision level.

RECORDS   The records and evidence of compliance are the signatures authorizing corrections and reissues of revised documents or, for electronic documents, signatures in document release logs or e-mails authorizing posting of documents on network.

AUDIT   Any handwritten corrections and notes on documents will alert auditors and prompt further investigation. Approved corrections are acceptable, but the approval must be given by an authorized person. If there is more than one copy of the document, all must be corrected in the same way.

REQUIREMENT   *Identify changes and current revision status of documents.*

IMPLEMENTATION   Documents should be directly identified with their revision level. Consecutive numbering using numerals or letters is the most common method. Sometimes the revision level may be included in the code identifying the document, or the date of issue may be used as the indication of the revision level.

There must also be a system for verifying what should be the latest revision level of a given document. The most common method is a master list of issued documents. For this purpose, the list need only specify the latest revision of a document, however, to help comply with other document control requirements the list could also provide such additional information as the date of issue, identification of the issuing authority, and distribution of the document. Document master lists can be maintained on electronic databases, catalog cards, or manual logs.

When relevant, changes in documents should be highlighted or otherwise identified. It cannot be assumed that the recipients of revised documents will engage in a systematic comparative analysis of the new and the old document to detect where changes were made. The most common way to identify changes is to summarize them on distribution cover sheets or transmittal letters, if used. Less formal methods — highlighting, marking on margins, or identifying changes on self-stick notes, for example — are also acceptable, but they should be documented and authorized.

DOCUMENTATION The general document control procedure should have a section dealing with revision status identification and control. The procedure should define how revision levels are identified on documents, how to verify the current revision level for a given document, and how to identify changes in documents.

RECORDS The records and evidence of compliance are provided by the documents themselves, displaying their revision level (or date of issue) and highlighting changes; and by master lists (or equivalent) providing the means for verifying the current revision status of documents.

AUDIT When assessing compliance, auditors will check if documents display their revision levels and how changes are identified, and will review the master lists or logs of issued documents. Auditors will also test the system for verifying revision status. They will pick a sample of documents from different locations around the company, note their revision levels, and ask someone to verify that these revision levels are indeed the last issued.

REQUIREMENT

Ensure that current documents are available at locations where they are used.

IMPLEMENTATION

There are two issues in this requirement. One is identification of the locations where specific documents should be available, and the other is effective distribution of the documents. Documents having permanent or fairly constant distribution should have distribution lists. The lists can be printed on the documents themselves or be maintained separately.

When distribution cannot be predicted in advance, documents can be made available on an as-needed basis. But their use must be recorded so that it is known where to follow up with revisions. If maintaining such a record is not practical, documents should be destroyed promptly or returned after one-time use. Any filing or storage of documents that cannot be automatically replaced with new revisions must be prohibited.

DOCUMENTATION

The general document control procedure should have a section dedicated to distribution of documents. The procedure should explain how distribution lists are documented and maintained, and what methods are used to physically deliver documents to their destinations. It should also explain, if applicable, how to use letters of transmittal, sign-off logs, or other means for confirmation of receipt. This procedure can be combined with the procedure regulating withdrawal of obsolete documents from points of use (see next requirement).

RECORDS

Distribution lists are the main evidence that the locations where documents must be placed are identified. The actual distribution of documents can be recorded in letters of transmittal, distribution logs, or simply by checkmarks on a distribution list. Any method is acceptable as long as it is documented in procedures. Document receipt records are not required, and should be used only where this is a contractual or regulatory requirement.

AUDIT

Assessing compliance, auditors will review the distribution lists and records, and test the distribution system. This can be done by either picking a name from a distribution list and verifying that the person indeed has the document; or the other way around, by picking up a document from somebody's file and verifying that the person is on the document's distribution list.

REQUIREMENT

Remove obsolete documents from points of use and identify retained copies of obsolete documents to prevent unintended use.

IMPLEMENTATION

Obsolete documents are usually removed from points of use at the same time that new revisions of the documents are distributed. There are basically two possibilities. Either superseded documents are exchanged for revised versions, or the recipients of revised documents are obliged to destroy the old copies. Direct exchange is more effective, of course, but the second method is also acceptable, provided that it can be satisfactorily implemented.

When historical documents need to be retained for preservation of knowledge or legal reasons, they should be stamped OBSOLETE or HISTORY, and be kept separate from current documents to preclude unintended use.

DOCUMENTATION

The general document control procedure should have a section dedicated to withdrawal and handling of obsolete documents. The procedure should explain the method used for withdrawal of obsolete documents, and prohibit unauthorized filing and storage of obsolete documents and any documents that are at risk of becoming obsolete because they are not automatically updated with new revisions. The procedure should also explain how historical copies of obsolete documents are identified and stored.

RECORDS   There are normally no records or other written evidence that obsolete documents are being withdrawn from points of use, unless a document distribution system includes logging of withdrawn documents. Identification of historical copies of obsolete documents would be evident on the documents themselves.

AUDIT   Because there are generally no records or other written evidence, compliance will be assessed by auditing and testing the system. Auditors will check documents against their master lists and will look for multiple revisions of a document in files and points of use. Auditors will also review samples of obsolete historical documents to verify that they are properly identified and, where relevant, are stored separately from current documents.

REQUIREMENT   *Ensure that documents of external origin are identified, and control their distribution.*

IMPLEMENTATION   Documents of external origin may be drawings, specifications, manuals, standards, regulations, contracts, etc. In fact, any document that is not established within or for the organization is an external document. Obviously not all external documents need to be controlled. Clause 4.2.3 applies only to those external documents that directly define product requirements and instruct how to carry out product realization processes and other operational activities. If an error in an external document or a mix-up of revision levels could result in product nonconformity, the document must be controlled.

Control of external documents need only include their identification, revision level, and distribution. There is no requirement for review and approval of external documents, although this may be relevant in some special cases.

DOCUMENTATION The general document control procedure should explicitly state in its scope of application that it also applies to relevant external documents, and it should have a dedicated section or clause to explain any special methods or differences that would only apply to external documents.

RECORDS The records and evidence of compliance are provided by the documents themselves, displaying their identification (name) and revision level or date of issue; by master lists (or equivalent) providing the means for verifying the current revision status of documents; and by distribution lists or letters of transmittal.

AUDIT Auditors will expect relevant external documents to be controlled in the same way, or to the same degree, as comparable internal documents (except for review and approval).

4.2.4   Control of Records

REQUIREMENT *Establish records as necessary to provide evidence of conformity to product and/or customer requirements and of the effective operation of the quality system.*

IMPLEMENTATION The first part of this requirement, pertaining to evidence of product conformity, refers to product verification and acceptance records and, where applicable, to records of qualification and monitoring of production (product realization) processes.

The second part of this requirement obliges organizations to ensure that they have sufficient evidence (records) to demonstrate that their quality system complies with ISO 9001 and that it is effective. The pertinent records are, first of all, reports of internal and external audits of the quality system and records of management reviews, and also other records providing evidence that all activities (processes) of the quality system are carried out according to requirements and planned arrangements.

DOCUMENTATION   The quality manual should confirm and communicate the policy that the scope of records should be sufficient to provide evidence of product and system conformity.

RECORDS   The evidence of compliance is a list of records, or categories of records, maintained by the organization. Such list is usually included in the operational procedure dealing with records (refer to the last requirement in this section).

AUDIT   This requirement, and especially the second part pertaining to quality system records, gives auditors the authority to request records or other evidence of compliance, and to issue findings when adequate records are not maintained. There is no intent here to oblige organizations to keep records for the sole purpose of proving their innocence. However, the standard in this clause also recognizes that verification of compliance is not possible without adequate records.

REQUIREMENT   *Index and organize records to facilitate their retrieval.*

IMPLEMENTATION   Section 4.2.4 specifically requires a procedure defining controls for identification, storage, protection, retrieval, retention, and disposition of records. All these words really mean one thing: retrievability. Any record management system is acceptable as long as it works. When a record has to be retrieved, it should be easily found, be legible, and in good condition.

Records should be filed and stored in designated locations. Cabinets, drawers, shelves, and files containing records should be clearly labeled. Electronic records must be backed up and all storage media must be labeled and protected against damage and deterioration. Records should be arranged and indexed by product, process, person, or event to which they pertain. When appropriate, the indexing should be cross-referenced. Specific functions (persons) should be assigned the responsibility for maintaining records.

DOCUMENTATION The operational procedure dealing with control of quality records should explain the policies and requirements for indexing, filing, and maintaining records, and should assign the responsibilities for these activities. Preservation and retrievability of records should be the ultimate objective of the record management system.

RECORDS There are no records required in this section. The evidence of compliance consists of the procedures and the implementation of the record management system.

AUDIT The functioning of the record management system is continuously tested throughout the whole audit. Auditors will ask for retrieval of records when assessing almost any activity of the quality system. Records are often the only evidence that certain activities are taking place (e.g., management reviews, design reviews, internal audits, corrective actions, training, etc.).

Auditors will pay attention to how long it takes to retrieve a record. It is not productive to have the auditor wait when a record cannot be located. If this happens, it is better to tell the auditor right away that there will be a delay in retrieving the record, so that the audit may continue while the record is being located.

When a record cannot be located at all, auditors will usually investigate the reason. If the problem is the lack of proper indexing and organization of records, there may be two findings: one for the audited activity (lack of evidence of compliance), and the other for the breakdown of the record management system.

REQUIREMENT *Determine and document retention times and storage locations for records.*

IMPLEMENTATION Retention times for records should be determined based on a commonsense consideration of how long the record may be relevant and useful. For example, product-related records should be retained for a period of time corresponding to the useful life of the product. Records pertaining to qualification and monitoring of subcontractors should be retained for as long as the subcontractor is used and/or the parts supplied by the subcontractor are active. Retention period for training records can be established on the basis of employment status, and so forth. Records pertaining to periodical assessments, reviews, and certifications, such as internal quality audit reports, management review records, or calibration certificates, are usually kept for three cycles, i.e., records of annual events are kept for three years.

To simplify the system, some companies determine one retention time for all records — five or ten years, for example — irrespective of whether the record pertains to product, quality system, or other activity or event. It is OK as long as this policy is not applied to records for which such fixed retention time would not make any sense, for example, personnel training records.

Records may be stored anywhere and by any department, as long as the location is known and is documented.

DOCUMENTATION   The procedure dealing with the control of records should list all relevant categories of records and stipulate for each the retention time and storage location. For those categories of records whose disposition depends on an event rather than passage of time, the retention period can be defined in terms of the event instead of absolute time. For example, the procedure can require that training records be retained for two years after termination of employment.

RECORDS   The evidence of compliance consists of procedures documenting retention times and storage locations for records, and the actual implementation of these retention requirements.

AUDIT   Assessing compliance, auditors will review the procedure stipulating retention times and storage locations for records and, to test the system, will ask for retrieval of some older records from various categories.

5 MANAGEMENT RESPONSIBILITY

5.1   MANAGEMENT COMMITMENT

REQUIREMENT   *Demonstrate top management commitment to the development and improvement of the quality system.*

IMPLEMENTATION   Specifically, this clause requires the top management to communicate the importance of meeting customer and regulatory requirements, establish quality policy and quality objectives, conduct management reviews, and ensure availability of resources.

The requirement is only for providing evidence of commitment. Therefore, there is really nothing to implement. Top management commitment will be demonstrated automatically through related activities, requirements for which are defined in other clauses of the standard. The relevant clauses are: 5.2, Customer Focus; 5.3, Quality Policy; 5.4, Planning; 5.5.2, Management Representative; 5.6, Management Review; and 6.2.2, Competence, Awareness and Training.

Identifying and meeting customer requirements is the principal theme of ISO 9000:2000. This obligation for the top management to communicate the importance of meeting customer requirements initiates a long series of requirements related to customer needs and expectations, customer satisfaction, customer communication, and customer-related processes.

DOCUMENTATION   The quality manual should explicitly state the commitment of the top management to all items listed in this clause, and should define management responsibilities in these areas.

RECORDS

To provide evidence of its commitment, the top management should be actively involved in establishing, maintaining, and reviewing the quality system. This involvement would be automatically reflected in various types of records and reports, in particular in management review records.

AUDIT

Throughout the whole audit the auditors will pay attention to any evidence of management involvement and commitment. It often shows up in little things like participation in quality-related meetings, being on distribution lists of documents pertaining to quality, recognition of personnel contributing to the advancement of the quality system, and so forth. But the most direct evidence of management commitment will emerge from the audit of management reviews of the quality system (refer to Clause 5.6).

5.2   CUSTOMER FOCUS

REQUIREMENT

Ensure that customer requirements are determined and are met, with the aim of enhancing customer satisfaction.

IMPLEMENTATION

This clause is redundant and unnecessary. The two issues it addresses — customer requirements and customer satisfaction — are already addressed much more specifically in Clause 7.2.1 and Clause 8.2.1, respectively.

In draft versions of the standard this clause used to require a system for determining customer needs and expectations. This worthwhile requirement was taken out from the final version, leaving just this fancy heading and the redundant and meaningless sentence filling the space below.

DOCUMENTATION

Although this requirement is not auditable (at least not under this clause), it should be acknowledged with a corresponding policy statement in the quality manual.

RECORDS   The evidence that customer requirements have been determined is the same as in Clause 7.2.1., while evidence of meeting those requirements would be generated in response to Clause 8.2.4. Evidence of customer satisfaction is required in Clause 8.2.1.

AUDIT   Auditors will not give much attention to this clause, as they would always prefer to audit against more specific requirements in other clauses that cover the same issues. The new and interesting aspect is only the title of this clause, Customer Focus, but auditors do not audit against titles.

5.3   QUALITY POLICY

REQUIREMENT   *Formulate a quality policy and ensure that it includes commitments to meeting requirements and to continual improvement.*

IMPLEMENTATION The quality policy should be formulated by the top executive management of the organization, usually the president, chairman, or owner of the company.

Technically, to comply with this requirement it is sufficient to insert somewhere in the text of the quality policy the key words *customer requirements* and *continual improvement*. However, while formulating the policy, companies should not focus solely on compliance, but try to express their true aspirations. The policy must not be just a nice-sounding but meaningless phrase, since it has an important role to play in the quality system. It must define the overarching goals for the quality system to achieve and provide a framework for more specific objectives (refer to the next requirement).

DOCUMENTATION   The quality policy must be documented (Clause 4.2.1.a). This is usually done in the quality manual, either under Section 5.3 or in a special section at the front of the manual.

RECORDS   The evidence of compliance is the quality policy itself.

AUDIT   Auditors will review the quality policy very carefully. They will look for clear commitments to meeting requirements and continual improvement, and will try to identify any additional commitments or goals expressed in the policy. In their minds, auditors will reduce the policy to a list of specific objectives. This will help them to determine whether the policy is appropriate, and if the quality system is adequate to fulfill the policy.

REQUIREMENT   *Ensure that the quality policy provides a framework for establishing and reviewing quality objectives.*

IMPLEMENTATION   To create a framework for setting and reviewing quality objectives, the quality policy must define broad and general goals from which more detailed objectives can be derived. For example, a general policy commitment to improve on-time delivery would create a framework for all objectives relevant to meeting delivery schedules.

The relationship between the quality policy and quality objectives is the best indicator of whether the quality policy is relevant or not. For example, if there are several objectives supporting a company-wide effort to improve on-time delivery, but the policy doesn't include any statements that would lead or even relate to this effort, auditors could conclude that the quality policy is irrelevant to what the company is actually trying to achieve. In ISO 9001:2000 the quality policy is not permanent. It must be periodically reviewed and updated to be always in the forefront, leading and providing direction for the quality effort (refer to Clause 5.6).

DOCUMENTATION   The quality manual should acknowledge this requirement with a general statement that the quality policy creates the framework for quality objectives. This would usually be done either in the same section where the quality policy is documented, or in the section dealing with quality objectives.

RECORDS

In this case, it is the documents — quality policy and objectives — rather than records that provide the primary evidence of compliance, although management review records are also relevant.

AUDIT

Auditors will analyze the quality policy and quality objectives to determine whether the general goals expressed in the policy provide a framework for the more specific objectives. Although, on intuitive level, this determination should be quite easy to make, auditors will not be able to support their conclusions with objective evidence. The auditee can argue that, for example, a policy commitment to customer satisfaction creates a framework for all their quality objectives. There is no support for an auditor to contradict such statement.

REQUIREMENT

Communicate and explain the quality policy within the organization.

IMPLEMENTATION

In addition to documenting the quality policy in the quality manual, the policy must be explicitly communicated and explained to all personnel.

The quality policy can be communicated on banners or posters displayed in conspicuous locations throughout the company, or in flyers or cards distributed to all employees. Explanation of the policy is usually included in the general orientation training for the quality system. Such training is otherwise required under Clause 6.2.2.

DOCUMENTATION

On the documentation level, it is sufficient to express in the quality manual a general commitment to communicate and explain the quality policy to all personnel within the organization. There is no need for procedures or other documentation explaining in detail how this will be done.

RECORDS

The evidence of compliance consists of the actual banners, posters, or cards with the quality policy; and personnel training records of the general quality system orientation training.

AUDIT Auditors will verify compliance by noting how the policy is communicated, by reviewing personnel training records, and by direct interviews with employees. Auditors will ask employees to explain what the quality policy means, and how they contribute in their work to fulfilling the policy. In these interviews auditors will also verify compliance with requirements of Clause 6.2.2 pertaining to awareness of the quality system.

REQUIREMENT *Periodically review the quality policy for continuing suitability.*

IMPLEMENTATION This requirement for periodical review of the quality policy is in line with the role of the policy. In order to provide direction for the quality system and create a framework for quality objectives, the policy must be current.

The quality policy is usually reviewed within the scope of management reviews. This is explicitly required in Clause 5.6. Every management review must consider the policy, and change it when it is no longer relevant or sufficient, or when goals and aspirations expressed in the policy have been attained.

DOCUMENTATION In the quality manual section dealing with the quality policy there should be some general statements confirming the commitment to periodically review the policy. There should also be a reference to the management review procedure, where the review process would be defined in more detail.

RECORDS To demonstrate compliance, the management review records should indicate that the quality policy is regularly reviewed for continuing suitability.

AUDIT Auditors will examine management review records to assure themselves that the quality policy is on the agenda of every review. They will also expect that the policy is actually changed from time to time in response to changing circumstances.

5.4   PLANNING

5.4.1   Quality Objectives

REQUIREMENT   *Establish measurable quality objectives at relevant functions and levels within the organization.*

IMPLEMENTATION In a nutshell, this requirement obliges the organization to set specific, measurable goals that will lead to the fulfillment of the quality policy and will provide contents for the commitments to meet requirements and to continual improvement.

To implement this requirement organizations must develop specific and measurable quality objectives. While the standard does not explicitly require an actual list of such objectives, a formal list authorized by the top management would be most convincing, at least for objectives pertaining to the general quality system and continual improvement. Objectives for product quality are usually documented in technical specifications, drawings, or contracts.

Quality objectives must be measurable. This means that an objective should be formulated in such a way that it is possible to measure progress toward attainment of the objective, and it is possible to determine when the objective has been reached. In practice, this usually implies specific numerical targets. For example, attainment of a specific, measurable product characteristic; or an objective to decrease rejects by a specific number or percentage. In some cases defining a measurable target will not be as obvious: for example, as in an objective to improve customer communication. Special rating or scoring systems will have to be developed for measuring such objectives.

Quality objectives must support the quality policy and be established at relevant functions and levels within the organization. This means that all functions and levels that are relevant to reaching a particular policy goal should contribute to reaching the goal through attainment of their particular objectives. For example, if the goal is to improve on-time delivery, all functions that have significant influence on maintaining the delivery schedule should have defined objectives to improve performance in their areas of responsibility.

A good practical approach to quality objectives is to divide them into categories corresponding to various modes of quality and continual improvement planning. With this approach, quality planning becomes a more practical and focused process aiming to define the methods, means, and resources needed to achieve specific objectives. For example, general quality planning (Clause 5.4.2) will be focused on objectives for the quality system; planning of product realization (Clause 7.1) and planning of product measurement and monitoring (Clause 8.2.4) will be driven by quality objectives for products; and planning for continual improvement (Clause 8.5.1) will be based on objectives for improving products, processes, or the quality system.

DOCUMENTATION   The quality manual should define the process and assign responsibilities for identifying and establishing quality objectives. This would normally be included in the section dealing with general quality planning (Clause 5.4). There is usually no need for a dedicated operational procedure instructing how to establish quality objectives. The procedure dealing with management reviews can address this issue, especially with regard to the review of programs for achieving quality objectives and establishment of new objectives.

RECORDS   The most convincing way to demonstrate compliance would be to have a list or a matrix of objectives authorized by the top management. But any way is acceptable as long as objectives are documented and authorized. There should also be some evidence of actions or projects for implementing the objectives.

AUDIT   Auditors will first verify that quality objectives are established and are measurable, and that there are some specific actions or projects being implemented to achieve the objectives. They will also want to evaluate whether quality objectives are consistent with the quality policy and whether they are established at all relevant functions and levels within the organization. However, it will not be easy to acquire solid objective evidence to support findings in those areas.

For this part of the audit, it is important that people escorting the auditors, or those being questioned, know exactly what the quality objectives are and how they are documented. They should also understand clearly the relationship between the quality objectives and the quality policy, and the relationship between the objectives and continual improvement actions. This can quickly get quite abstract and confusing, especially where quality objectives are defined and documented in many different ways, such as engineering changes, preventive actions, improvement projects, etc.

5.4.2   Quality Management System Planning

REQUIREMENT   *Plan processes and resources required for the quality system and for achieving quality objectives.*

IMPLEMENTATION   ISO 9001:2000 has a different approach to quality planning than the previous editions. In the 2000 edition, quality planning is addressed in four separate clauses:

- Clause 5.4.2 — Planning for achievement of quality objectives and general quality system planning;
- Clause 7.1 — Planning of product realization processes and product verification and validation activities;
- Clause 7.3.1 — Design and/or development planning; and
- Clause 8.1 — Planning of measurement and monitoring of products, processes, quality system performance, and customer satisfaction.

Only the first planning element (Clause 5.4.2) will be discussed here. Other elements will be addressed under their respective clauses.

Planning of the quality management system is implemented through the process of drafting the quality manual. The manual identifies processes (elements) comprising the quality system, and describes methods and means necessary for implementing the system.

Planning for achieving quality objectives is best done by establishing special management programs for reaching the objectives and monitoring progress. However, as this is not explicitly required in the standard, some lesser methods would probably be sufficient; for example, an action item in minutes of a management review.

DOCUMENTATION The quality manual should outline the process and assign responsibilities for quality planning in all relevant aspects, and for updating quality plans in response to changes.

An operational procedure for quality planning is not explicitly required, and would not be needed as long as the manual is sufficiently explicit in defining the overall system. However, if planning for achieving the quality objectives involves establishment of special management programs and monitoring systems, a procedure could be warranted. It would instruct how to define and document methods, resources, responsibilities, and time frames for achieving objectives; and how progress toward achieving objectives is to be monitored. A common format for initiating and defining simple management programs is a one-page program brief (or kickoff sheet). It is often established using a special form, similar to forms used for initiating corrective and preventive actions. The form may also have blocks for monitoring progress and closing out the program. For more complex programs there would usually be a whole file with different documents for planning the program and recording its performance.

RECORDS The output of quality management system planning is the quality manual, which in itself is the primary evidence of this activity.

Planning for achieving quality objectives is best documented in management program briefs (or kickoff sheets) that define the methods, resources, responsibilities, and time frames for these programs. However, a lesser documentation may be sufficient; for example, an action item in a management review record or a reference to an existing procedure.

AUDIT

As long as there is a complete quality manual, auditors will have a difficult time finding objective evidence of insufficient quality system planning. But to be sure, auditors must be told explicitly that the manual is the actual output of the quality planning process.

Planning for achievement of quality objectives is much more vulnerable. Here, for every objective, the auditor may ask: What are the plans for achieving this objective? The best answer would be to point out a specific project or program with defined responsibilities, means, methods, resources, and time frame. But a less specific response may also be acceptable, such as pointing to a general procedure of the quality system that would broadly support the objective. For example, if additional training is the way for achieving an objective, the general training procedure would define the methods, means, and resources for reaching the objective, and there would be no need for developing any special new programs.

REQUIREMENT

Maintain the integrity of the quality system when changes to the system are planned and implemented.

IMPLEMENTATION

This requirement recognizes that in a quality management system all processes, elements, and activities must interact properly and work together to produce the desired result. There is a real danger that changes may throw the system out of balance and cause breakdowns.

There are two issues here. One is changes to the quality system in response to changing circumstances, such as the introduction of new products or technology, plant relocation, and expansion or contraction of capacity. The other is changes to improve the quality system, i.e., make it more effective. It is the first category that creates the biggest risk.

The most practical way to comply is to include a review of quality system changes in the management reviews, and to develop a policy that all significant changes in the company should be evaluated with respect to their impact on the quality system (much in the same way as new projects are often evaluated with respect to environmental impacts).

DOCUMENTATION The quality manual should express a general commitment to protect the integrity of the quality system while planning and implementing changes. In addition, the operational procedure for management reviews should require that quality system changes always be included in the review. It could also be relevant to develop and document a policy stating that all new projects and other major changes must be evaluated with respect to their impact on the quality system.

RECORDS The primary records are minutes or reports from management reviews. Additional evidence of compliance would be provided by memos, reports, or other communication showing that the integrity of the quality system was indeed considered when introducing a new product or technology or other changes.

AUDIT It is questionable whether this requirement can be audited effectively, because it is inherently difficult to establish, and to acquire evidence, that management does not ensure the integrity of the quality system during changes. Such conclusion can only be made with certainty when there is actual evidence of system breakdown caused by inadequate planning or implementation of changes.

Nonetheless, auditors will ask the question and will expect some systemic arrangements demonstrating implementation of this requirement. The most common way is having quality system changes included in the agenda of management reviews.

5.5 RESPONSIBILITY, AUTHORITY AND COMMUNICATION

5.5.1 Responsibility and Authority

REQUIREMENT *Define and communicate responsibilities and authorities within the organization.*

IMPLEMENTATION Organizational charts should be prepared depicting key personnel whose work affects quality and who have the authority and responsibility to identify and correct nonconformities, verify implementation of corrective actions, and control nonconforming product.

The charts are to define organizational units (departments and functions) and their interrelation. Although the standard refers only to that part of the organization concerned with the quality system, it is customary to include all departments. In larger companies, the general organizational chart can be supplemented by more detailed charts depicting the internal organizations of the QA and/or QC departments.

Quality-related responsibilities of each department should be clearly defined to include responsibilities for specific quality system processes (process owners).

The organizational charts and the quality-related responsibilities should reflect that managers who are responsible for quality have sufficient authority and have unobstructed and unrestricted access to the executive management.

DOCUMENTATION There is no need to have a special operational procedure to comply with this requirement. The organizational charts and specifications of departmental responsibilities are usually included in the quality manual. In addition, specific responsibilities for particular activities would be defined in operational procedures that regulate these activities.

RECORDS The evidence of compliance includes organizational charts, job descriptions, and assignments of specific responsibilities and authorities in the quality manual and operational procedures. Implementation is evidenced by various records and authorizations demonstrating that those persons appointed with specific responsibilities and authorities are indeed actively involved.

AUDIT   When assessing compliance, auditors will review the quality manual, operational procedures, and job descriptions (if available) to verify that responsibilities and authorities for all functions and activities affecting the quality system are clearly defined. Auditors would normally never question the organizational structure, as there are no longer any requirements in the standard regarding the organizational interrelation. The only requirement is for defining and communicating the organizational structure, whatever it may be.

5.5.2   Management Representative

REQUIREMENT   *Appoint a management representative for the quality system.*

IMPLEMENTATION   Vice president, director, or manager of quality assurance is a natural choice for the management representative. However, if such function does not exist or there are other reasons for appointing someone else, anyone from the management may be appointed irrespective of his or her other responsibilities. It is not required that the representative be actively involved in the day-to-day operations of the quality system. This person should have a direct access to the top executive manager of the organization, and should assume the authority for directing the quality system.

The standard explicitly lists three areas of responsibility and authority the management representative must have: (1) ensuring that the quality system is properly established, implemented and maintained; (2) reporting to the top management on the performance of the quality system and any need for improvement; and (3) ensuring the promotion of awareness of customer requirements throughout the organization.

DOCUMENTATION The appointment of the management representative and the authority and responsibilities of this function should be documented, usually in the quality manual.

RECORDS The record and evidence of compliance consists of the documented appointment itself, and of the evidence that the management representative is actively exercising his or her authority.

AUDIT When assessing compliance, auditors will verify that the management representative is appointed, and that the representative is actively involved in implementing and maintaining the quality system, reporting to management, and ensuring awareness of customer requirements. The involvement will manifest itself in various records demonstrating that the representative participates in meetings, issues directives, generates reports, approves documents, and so forth.

Auditors will also look for specific evidence that customer requirements and the importance of meeting these requirements are communicated to all personnel. This could be in a form of training, a bulletin board posting, an intranet site, etc.

In most companies the management representative is also responsible for interfacing with the registrar. In all matters regarding ISO 9000 certification, and during any certification audit, auditors will look to the management representative for making appropriate arrangements to receive the audit and for making pertinent decisions, resolving problems, signing documents, and otherwise interfacing with the auditors.

5.5.3   Internal Communication

REQUIREMENT *Ensure effective internal communication regarding the quality management system.*

IMPLEMENTATION This requirement refers to arrangements and systems to ensure that quality policies, objectives, procedures, instructions, records, data, and other information regarding the quality management system are effectively communicated throughout the organization.

Obviously, every company already uses various methods for internal communication, but they may not be formally identified and managed. Typical elements of such communication systems are documents, records, meetings, reviews, quality-related training, team briefings, bulletin boards, intranet sites, suggestion boxes, and so forth. There is no intent in this requirement to reorganize internal communication into one, centralized system. But the existing elements must be coordinated and formally managed.

Formal management of communication is usually achieved through document control procedures; planning and scheduling of meetings and reviews, and recording their results; planning, providing, and recording training; assigning responsibilities (and possibly developing procedures) for maintenance of bulletin boards and/or intranet sites, and so forth.

DOCUMENTATION The quality manual should identify internal communication systems, assign responsibilities for establishing and maintaining the systems, and define in general how communication is managed. There should be also references to relevant procedures.

The standard does not require a procedure for the overall management of the internal communication system, but requires documented procedures for some of its elements, in particular for document control and for control of records. Other procedures may be developed as required, for example, for training, management reviews, or maintenance of bulletin boards and intranet sites.

In addition, various procedures and instructions dealing with particular activities should specify how information and data generated by the activity is to be recorded and distributed. For example, the procedure for control of nonconforming product should specify who receives copies of product nonconformity reports; and the procedure for internal audits should instruct on the distribution of internal audit findings.

RECORDS To demonstrate compliance, applicable communication systems should be identified, maintained, and managed. The evidence of compliance includes document distribution lists and records, training records, minutes of meetings and reviews, and so forth.

AUDIT Auditors will ask about and review the overall communication system, and will question employees about some important issues regarding the quality system to verify that the issues were effectively communicated. Everyone must know where to find and how to access relevant portions of the quality system documentation, and be aware of any other facility that is intended for communicating quality-related information (such as bulletin boards, newsletters, or intranet site).

5.6 MANAGEMENT REVIEW

5.6.1 General

REQUIREMENT *Periodically review the quality system to ensure its continuing suitability and effectiveness, and to identify the need for changes and opportunities for improvement.*

IMPLEMENTATION The executive management is required to periodically review the quality management system to identify the need for changes to the quality system, quality policy, and quality objectives, and to identify opportunities for improvement. The purpose of the reviews is to ensure continuing suitability and effectiveness of the quality system. Suitability and effectiveness of the system should be judged on the basis of its ability to achieve objectives stated in the quality policy.

The requirement for evaluating the need to change the quality policy and objectives reinforces the concept that the quality policy is a set of aspirations and commitments for the quality system to achieve, rather than a marketing slogan. Some people may feel uncomfortable with the quality policy being questioned at every management review meeting, but this is precisely what is now required.

The reviews must be conducted regularly. They may be scheduled quarterly, semi-annually or annually, based on the maturity level of the implemented quality system. It is a common practice to schedule reviews on a quarterly or semi-annual basis for the first year of operation and then reduce the frequency to annual. There should also be provisions for scheduling additional reviews in response to unforeseen events and developments, such as the addition of new technologies or products, relocation, or sudden and serious problems with quality performance.

The reviews can be in the form of meetings, telecommunication conferencing, or circulation of reports or memos. A meeting is the most popular and established way. All key executive managers who are responsible for or are affected by product quality should participate in the reviews, to include managers of marketing, customer service, engineering, production, quality assurance, and others as appropriate.

DOCUMENTATION The quality manual should include a policy commitment to periodically conduct management reviews of the quality system and a general outline of this process. Specifics, such as the agenda, attendance, and scheduling, should be documented in an operational procedure. The procedure should also instruct how to prepare records of management reviews.

RECORDS Management reviews must be recorded. The format of the record will depend on the nature of the review itself. Records could include minutes of meetings; memos from the executive management; reports with findings, conclusions, and timetables for implementing resolutions and actions; and so forth. Storage location and retention period for the records should be specified in a procedure. These management review records should be properly established and maintained as they are the only evidence of compliance on which auditors will base their assessment.

AUDIT To assess compliance, auditors will carefully examine the management review records and will interview management personnel who participate in the

reviews. Auditors will verify that the reviews are conducted in accordance with the established frequency
and schedules, that all relevant managers participate, and that all required items and issues are covered. They will also verify that the conclusions and recommendations of the reviews are being implemented.

5.6.2   Review Input

REQUIREMENT   *Provide the management review with input information on the status and performance of the quality system, products, and processes, and recommendations for improvement.*

IMPLEMENTATION   This clause includes a list of specific items that must
be reviewed with regard to performance and improve-
ment opportunities. These are internal audits, customer feedback, process performance, product conformity, preventive and corrective actions, actions from
previous reviews, changes that could affect the quality system, and recommendations for improvement.

DOCUMENTATION   The management review procedure (if such is established) should require that all items listed in this
clause be included in the agenda of management
reviews. The procedure may also assign specific
responsibilities and a format for presenting various
items. Thus, for example, the customer service manager may be assigned to present information, data,
and statistics related to customer feedback; while the
quality assurance manager would present data pertaining to corrective and preventive actions.

RECORDS   Management review agenda, minutes, and output
records should demonstrate that all items required in
this clause were presented and evaluated, and conclusions were recorded.

AUDIT   To verify compliance, auditors will examine the agenda and records of the review to assure themselves
that all input items required in Clause 5.6.2 were
addressed. Where appropriate, auditors will also ask

for the materials that were presented at the review. This is especially relevant with regard to information and data that are explicitly required elsewhere in the standard; for example, the quality performance data that is required in Clause 8.4, Analysis of Data.

5.6.3 Review Output

REQUIREMENT *Include in the management review output actions related to improvement of the quality system, products, and resource needs.*

IMPLEMENTATION This clause requires every management review to be concluded with actions to improve the effectiveness of the quality system and product conformity to customer requirements, along with commitment of necessary resources to implement these actions.

Implementation of this requirement will be natural for companies that already use the management review to improve themselves and their products. All that is required here is an action to improve an unsatisfactory condition, and allocation of necessary resources to implement the action. This already happens in every company, but not always within the framework of management reviews.

Improvement of the effectiveness of the quality system can manifest itself as a revision of a procedure, addition of a work instruction, establishment of a new training program, process improvement, or establishment of new or improved methods for product verification or testing. Anything that makes the quality system more effective and efficient can be credited.

Improvement of product related to customer requirements can take form of improved on-time delivery performance, shorter delivery cycles, tighter tolerances or better consistency of product characteristics, better product information, improved service or warranty conditions, redesigned product features or performance, or lower price — anything that adds value for the customer and increases customer satisfaction.

Allocation of resources may be the assignment of personnel to specific improvement projects, dedication of space and equipment, purchasing of materials, hiring of external consultants and experts, and providing training — anything that is necessary for the development and implementation of improvement projects. Every improvement action must be backed up by the commitment of necessary resources; and there must be a record of what specific resources were dedicated.

DOCUMENTATION The quality manual and the operational procedure dealing with management reviews should require that the reviews be concluded with actions to improve the quality system and products, and with the allocation of necessary resources.

RECORDS Management review minutes and/or other review output documents will provide evidence of compliance and implementation. Improvement actions do not necessarily need to be documented separately or otherwise emphasized, but they must be there somewhere in the review output documents — sometimes just by a reference to a corrective or preventive action, for example.

AUDIT Auditors will examine management review records to find evidence of specific actions for improving the quality system and improving products. They will also want to see specific allocation of resources for each action. For this part of the audit it is important that the management personnel are familiar with the concept of management review output and the pertinent requirements. Too often presidents and other executive managers are completely unaware that there are some specific ISO 9001 requirements for the scope of actions resulting from management reviews.

RESOURCE MANAGEMENT

6.1 PROVISION OF RESOURCES

REQUIREMENT *Determine and provide resources needed to implement, maintain, and improve the quality system, and to enhance customer satisfaction.*

IMPLEMENTATION Resources required for the quality system are usually limited to personnel, management, and administrative support. However, resources required for meeting customer requirements are virtually all the resources that the company needs to operate, because the purpose for everything the company does is, in fact, meeting customer requirements and enhancing customer satisfaction. Thus, the requirement here is for determining and providing all necessary resources, including know-how, technology, processing equipment, personnel, infrastructure, supporting services, and anything else required to operate the company.

DOCUMENTATION To satisfy this requirement on the documentation level, it is sufficient to state in the quality manual that the management is committed to providing adequate resources for maintaining and improving the quality system and for meeting customer requirements.

RECORDS No special records or other documentary evidence of compliance is required. There is no requirement for formal allocation of resources, such as budgets. The adequacy of deployed resources will be judged on the basis of the overall performance of the quality system.

AUDIT This is obviously an important requirement, but not readily auditable. Even when auditors can clearly see that there are insufficient staff and/or other resources to maintain the quality system, they will often find it difficult to support their observation with specific objective evidence. In any event, to cite inadequate resources is very confrontational. Instead, auditors usually prefer to identify those nonconformities that are caused by inadequate resources, rather than citing directly the inadequacy of resources itself. For example, when corrective actions are not followed up in a timely manner due to inadequate staffing, the resulting finding will usually just refer to the delay itself, without mentioning the underlying lack of resources.

6.2 HUMAN RESOURCES

6.2.1 General

6.2.2 Competence, Awareness and Training

REQUIREMENT *Determine the necessary competence for personnel performing work affecting product quality.*

IMPLEMENTATION In this requirement, companies are asked to determine the minimum level of eduction, training, experience, and other qualifications for all personnel performing work affecting product quality. Although, theoretically, one can argue that this pertains to all personnel without exceptions, in practice the focus is on personnel directly involved in product realization (production) and product verification (inspection and testing).

A common way to implement this requirement is for every department to have a matrix associating all relevant functions, positions, and operations with qualification requirements, and identifying qualification status of all personnel in the department. In such a matrix, the first column lists functions, positions, and operations; the second column specifies corresponding qualification requirements; and each subsequent column is used for identifying the qualification status of the employees. For example, if the field at the intersection of the row for the punching press operation and the column for Mr. Green is crossed, this means that Mr. Green satisfies qualification requirements for operating the punching press.

The specification of qualification requirements can refer to education, experience, and specific skills. It can also refer to internal or external courses; training, certification or licensing; or passing certain tests or exams. For example, the qualification requirement for punching press operator may be four hours of instruction by an already qualified operator and completion of the safety training.

DOCUMENTATION   Although not explicitly required in the standard, a procedure dealing with competence, training, and awareness should be established in every company, except maybe in some very small organizations. The procedure would explain how competence requirements are determined and by whom, and how to document them.

RECORDS   The evidence of compliance is provided by documents defining qualification requirements for all employees whose work has a direct impact on product quality. These documents may be in any format, such as job specification/description sheets, or a competence matrix, as described above. Irrespective of format, these documents must be controlled in accordance with requirements of Clause 4.2.

AUDIT   Auditors will expect managers and supervisors to demonstrate that competence requirements for the positions in their departments are determined and are known. Although the standard does not explicitly require that this must be documented, in practice it will be very hard to convince auditors that someone's head is an appropriate and effective storage for this kind of information.

Auditors will also verify that the deployed personnel satisfy the competence requirements. They will do this by reviewing education, experience, training, and other qualification records of selected employees, and compare them against requirements.

REQUIREMENT   *Provide training or take other actions to ensure that personnel have the required level of knowledge, competence, and skill.*

IMPLEMENTATION   Once the level of required competence is established the next step is to provide training or undertake other actions to ensure that all personnel meet these requirements. Providing internal or external training is probably the most obvious method. But there can be other ways, for example, shifting underqualified personnel to other positions and hiring new people; or replacing old technology that required sophisticated skills with automated processes that do not require such skills. Whatever is done, the end result must be that personnel in all positions meet defined competence requirements.

Training can be provided in many ways. It can be a simple demonstration of how to operate a machine; on-the-job assistance and monitoring; practicing skills on samples and simulators; theoretical classroom lecturing; external courses and seminars; and self-study from books, articles, or video courses. Regardless of the form and duration, training should always be formally documented and recorded.

Training documentation should provide information about the content, scope, duration, and form of training. Based on the documentation alone, it should be possible to make an accurate assumption of what knowledge and skills can be expected from the trained person. Just mentioning the title of a course is not sufficient. Whenever possible, a copy of the materials used in training should be retained for documentation purposes.

DOCUMENTATION   The operational procedure dealing with training should outline the overall system for providing training in different areas and categories. It should also define for every category of training the requirements regarding instructor qualifications, documentation of content, and establishment of records.

RECORDS

Education, experience, and training records will be discussed in the last requirement of this section.

AUDIT

To assess compliance, auditors will review the training program, documentation specifying training content and format, and training records; and will interview personnel, asking how they learned the skills required in their positions. Auditors will also select a group of employees for more detailed examination of their education, experience, and training records, and will compare their level of qualifications against competence requirements for their positions.

REQUIREMENT

Evaluate the effectiveness of training provided or other actions taken.

IMPLEMENTATION

Effectiveness of training (or other actions to improve competency) should be evaluated for the specific training provided, rather than the overall training program. The best way to accomplish this is to define specific and, if possible, measurable objectives for each training, and then evaluate whether the objectives have been achieved.

The most direct way to evaluate the effectiveness of training is to measure on-the-job performance of employees, such as productivity or reject rates, for example, before and after training. But this is not always possible. When nonconformities caused by inadequate competence may be hidden (as in welding or casting), or the cost or consequences of failure are prohibitive (as in flying a plane), testing and certification on samples or simulators will be the only way to evaluate the effectiveness of training.

Another way to evaluate whether training was effective is to measure statistical improvement in performance of a whole group of employees or even the whole company. This would be the way, for example, to measure the effectiveness of safety training. Statistical decrease in the number or frequency of accidents will indicate that training was successful.

Individualized on-the-job training for a single employee or a small group — for example, instruction on how to operate a new machine — could be evaluated by a follow-up review conducted by the supervisor. If, say, for two weeks after the training was provided the employee did not have any problems with operating the machine, the training must have been effective. The record for such evaluation could be just a dated and signed note in the training record stating that the training was followed up and was determined to have been effective.

Training where there are no performance-related results that can be readily measured, such as training in communication skills, for example, can be concluded with a simple test just to check if the participants have absorbed the material, and then be followed up at a management review to discuss whether there is any noticeable improvement resulting from the training.

The standard does not name any preferred methods for evaluating the effectiveness of training, and auditors do not have any specific expectations. Any method that is sound and sincere will be acceptable.

DOCUMENTATION Methods for evaluating various types of training should be documented. The documentation should be as specific as possible, particularly for permanent training programs, such as routinely provided on-the-job training, safety, or general orientation. In smaller companies the evaluation methods can be documented directly in the training procedure. However, where the training program is more complex, a procedure could be easily overwhelmed, and a better way would be to document the evaluation methods in separate specifications for each training.

RECORDS Training evaluation records should be established and maintained. Typically, these are evaluation reports, scoring sheets, questionnaires, or records of reviews. The type and format of the record will depend on the evaluation method, and does not need to be the same for all types of training.

AUDIT   Auditors will go over the training program and will review the methods used for evaluating the effectiveness of training. They will select a sample of specific training events and will ask for records demonstrating that the effectiveness of this training was evaluated. Auditors will be alerted to superficial and obviously ineffective evaluation methods that have no practical value other than to help pass the audit.

REQUIREMENT   ***Ensure that employees are aware of the importance of their activities and how they contribute to the achievement of quality objectives.***

IMPLEMENTATION   The scope of employee awareness programs should cover general orientation about the quality system, discussion of the quality policy and quality objectives, explanation of procedures, and consequences of not following procedures. To satisfy Clauses 5.1, 5.2 and 5.5.2, the awareness program should also include communication of customer and regulatory requirements and explain the importance of meeting the requirements.

Awareness programs may be implemented through measures such as training, team briefings, newsletters, bulletin boards, or intranet site. Some of these systems were already discussed under Clause 5.5.3, Internal Communication. The program may have several components, with some of them targeted only to relevant groups of employees.

DOCUMENTATION   The quality manual should confirm the commitments to ensure that employees are aware of the importance of their activities, and of meeting customer requirements and achieving quality objectives; also that they understand how the quality management system will help to achieve these goals.

The training procedure should have a section dedicated to awareness programs: to define how these programs are initiated and approved, and by whom, and how are they documented, monitored, and reviewed.

RECORDS   All awareness-related training and other events should be recorded. Additional evidence may include banners, posters, bulletin board, or an intranet site.

AUDIT   In addition to reviewing awareness programs and events, auditors will interview individual employees to evaluate the level of their awareness. The questions may be, for example: What kinds of defects (nonconformities) could happen at your work station (process)? What would happen if those defects were not discovered and the product was passed on? Can you name any of the quality objectives that the company is now trying to achieve? Is your work important to achieving any of the objectives? How? To verify compliance with other clauses of the standard these interviews could also include questions about the quality policy, quality system documentation, or specific procedures that the employee should know.

REQUIREMENT *Maintain appropriate records of education, training, skills, and experience.*

IMPLEMENTATION Records of the initial qualifications of personnel commencing employment should be as complete as possible. These are typically résumés with photocopies of diplomas, certificates, recommendations, and other supporting documents.

The initial qualifications records are then supplemented by training records as the employee receives various types of training. These can include lists of training attendance, certificates, diplomas, licenses, or any other document evidencing that the person participated in training, passed a test, or otherwise satisfied requirements.

Companies preparing for ISO 9000 certification that previously did not have a formalized training system and did not keep training records can grandfather in their existing personnel. Instead of training records, managers or supervisors can issue certificates confirming the qualifications of their employees. These certifications must be justified, i.e., must reference specific reasons why the employee is considered to be qualified for a particular process or operation. Most often the justification is the actual experience of the employee with the process and a history of satisfactory performance.

DOCUMENTATION   Procedures, training briefs, or other documentation should specify what training records are to be established for particular types of training, where they should be kept, and for how long.

RECORDS   All forms of training should be recorded, including demonstrations, on-the-job training, and self-study. The records can be kept centrally, by the human resources department, for example, or be filed locally in the department where the employee works.

AUDIT   Auditors usually make notes about employees whom they interview or witness performing particular activities. When looking at training, the auditors will often ask for these employees' training records. Auditors will review the records to verify that the employees' qualifications meet requirements for the job they performed. Auditors will also verify that that the employees were provided with awareness training, such as general orientation about the quality system.

6.3   INFRASTRUCTURE

REQUIREMENT   *Provide and maintain infrastructure needed to achieve product conformity.*

IMPLEMENTATION   For the purpose of this clause, infrastructure is defined as buildings, work spaces, utilities, process equipment, software, computer networks, transportation, and other such supporting services.

Although there is no doubt that appropriate and properly maintained infrastructure is important, this clause is not readily auditable, except for maintenance of production equipment. The problem for auditors is to acquire objective evidence that the infrastructure is not adequate. Such evidence would have to demonstrate linkage between specific product non-conformities and inadequate infrastructure.

Equipment maintenance is much easier to audit, mainly because it was already required in the previous editions of ISO 9001 and in other quality system standards. As nothing specific is required, any coherent system for equipment maintenance is acceptable. To be credible, the system should focus on prevention. Typical elements of an equipment maintenance system are maintenance schedules, maintenance and repair manuals, replacement parts and supplies inventory, methods for verification of maintenance and repairs, and maintenance and repair records.

The maintenance plan can be a simple list or matrix specifying how often lubricants, seals, drive belts, and other supplies and parts need to be changed for each machine. Equipment manufacturers' maintenance manuals can be used directly to demonstrate that preventive maintenance requirements are defined.

DOCUMENTATION To acknowledge this clause, the quality manual should include some general statements of commitment to define, provide, and maintain suitable infrastructure. Where equipment maintenance is an important issue and these activities are organized into a separate department or unit, there should also be an operational procedure defining the equipment maintenance system. The procedures would instruct how to prepare the maintenance plan, what spare parts to stock, what are the servicing verification requirements, and what maintenance records must be established.

RECORDS The evidence of compliance consists of any records demonstrating that the infrastructure is adequate and is adequately maintained. These can be minutes of management meetings where infrastructure issues are discussed, maintenance contracts, and records of actual servicing and repairs. Where equipment maintenance is applicable, there will also be maintenance programs and servicing records.

AUDIT   The only time auditors will be able to write a finding against this clause (other than equipment maintenance) will be in places where infrastructure is literally broken — leaking roofs, broken windows, or broken equipment.

With regard to equipment maintenance, auditors will review the maintenance plans, noting if all relevant machines are included and if the plans are consistent with the equipment manufacturer's recommendations. Auditors will also review maintenance records to verify that the plans are consistently implemented.

6.4   WORK ENVIRONMENT

REQUIREMENT   *Determine and manage the work environment as needed to achieve product conformity.*

IMPLEMENTATION   At first, this clause may be interpreted as a movement of ISO 9000 into the realm of Health and Safety (H&S). However, careful reading reveals that in ISO 9001 the work environment is relevant only in the context of product conformity. To identify a finding against this clause, auditors must have objective evidence that working conditions are detrimental to achieving product conformity. Violation of health and safety regulations or standards would not in itself be sufficient to justify a finding.

The working environment may be specified in laws and regulations, in company H&S manuals and policies, in external standards and codes of practice to which the company subscribes (for example SA 8000), or even in contracts. In some instances it may also be appropriate to establish specific limits for particular processes, operations, or areas, irrespective of whether these are regulated or not. For example, a time limit on how long people may work inside freezers, maximum allowable temperature in areas where there are furnaces or other heat-emitting equipment, limits on allowable exposure to hazardous or potentially hazardous substances, noise limits, and so forth.

DOCUMENTATION The quality manual should include a commitment to define and provide a suitable work environment, and should reference relevant policies, procedures, and specifications (for example, the H&S manual).

There is usually no need for a dedicated procedure for defining and implementing an appropriate work environment.

RECORDS Typically, there will be no specific records demonstrating compliance. The evidence will emerge from interviews and general observation of existing conditions.

AUDIT This requirement is auditable only in situations where working conditions are obviously inappropriate, and in situations where there are actually specified requirements for work the environment.

Auditors will pay attention to work methods, ambient conditions, and other aspects of the work environment, and will ask whether there are specified limits on conditions that could impact quality performance.

Violations against any specified requirements, such as regulations, H&S procedures, or internal standards, may lead to a finding against this clause, but this will depend on the specific situation and its interpretation by the auditor. Strictly speaking, as long as the ability to achieve conformity of product is not compromised, auditors should not be able to write a finding against this clause.

7

PRODUCT REALIZATION

7.1   Planning of Product Realization

REQUIREMENT   *Establish documented quality plans for product realization processes and product validation activities.*

IMPLEMENTATION   This is the main clause in ISO 9001:2000 for what is traditionally understood as quality planning, i.e., establishment of plans for realization of a specific product and for verifying that the product conforms to specified requirements. Other aspects of quality planning are discussed under Clause 5.4.2, Quality Management System Planning.

Specifically, this clause requires organizations to determine:

- Quality objectives for products;
- The need for processes, facilities, documentation, and other resources required for product realization;
- Product verification and validation activities, and the criteria for acceptability; and
- The need for records to demonstrate product and process conformity.

These product-specific quality plans must be documented.

DOCUMENTATION   ISO 9001:2000 does not explicitly require a documented procedure for product realization and verification planning. However, as such procedure was required in previous editions of the standard, there is a certain expectation that it shall be established.

Developing quality plans for a product is a collaborative process involving many functions and departments, and there is often a real need for a procedure to coordinate and control this process. Such procedure would define the main phases, categories, and scope of product realization and verification planning; define how the plans are to be documented; and assign responsibilities for the planning and establishment of pertinent documents.

RECORDS

Plans for product realization activities are usually documented in product drawings and specifications, material or process flow diagrams, process flowcharts, work instructions, setup sheets, work orders, travellers, and any other such documents defining the means and methods of production. Plans for product verification may be documented in inspection and testing procedures, drawings and specifications, travellers, control plans, and any other such documents specifying the inspection and testing program for a given product. Collectively, these documents will provide the evidence of compliance with this clause.

AUDIT

To verifying compliance, auditors look for evidence that planning of product realization (production) is a well-defined and controlled process. They will be interested in such things as flowcharts, travellers, or other documents defining and sequencing all realization processes; testing and validation of production processes; process setup sheets; production trial runs; and work instructions. Not all of these things will be expected everywhere, but these are the types of issues that are relevant.

To verify planning of product verification, auditors will look for similar things, but in the area of inspection and testing. They will be interested in flowcharts, travellers or control plans defining and sequencing all verification activities for a product; inspection and testing procedures, to include methods and equipment to be used; acceptance criteria; and requirements for records.

7.2   CUSTOMER-RELATED PROCESSES

7.2.1   Determination of Requirements Related to Product

REQUIREMENT *Determine product requirements, to include customer requirements and requirements necessary for intended use and for compliance with laws and regulations.*

IMPLEMENTATION Customer requirements shall be understood broadly to include requirements for availability, delivery, and support.

The process for identifying customer requirements has a special strategic importance in ISO 9001:2000. Throughout the standard, customer requirements are the object of clauses related to management responsibility, quality policy and quality objectives, employee awareness, and many others. In fact, meeting customer requirements is set out in the standard as the principal objective of the quality management system. Obviously, before customer requirements can be met, they must be identified and determined. And that is the purpose of this clause.

Processes for identifying product requirements will vary significantly between industries and organizations. In the simplest case the process will practically boil down to a routine contract review, while on the other extreme there will be complex systems for researching customer needs and expectations, analyzing trends, examining competitive products, conducting surveys, market testing, and so forth.

Every company already has certain established activities related to the identification of product requirements. They are typically conducted by sales, marketing, customer service, and engineering functions. Implementation of this clause should start with identifying and reviewing these activities and documenting them in the quality manual and procedures. After the existing activities are documented and organized into a system, it will become apparent whether the system is sufficient or needs further improvements to comply with the requirements of this clause.

To ensure the integrity of the whole quality system, the process for determining product and customer requirements must be meaningful and effective, because outputs of this process will be used in many other elements of the system. Meeting customer requirements is the principal objective of the quality system.

DOCUMENTATION It is generally sufficient to outline the process for determining customer and/or product requirements in the quality manual alone. This is true especially for subcontractors supplying materials, components, or parts to precise customer specifications. However, where this process is more complex — for example, in organizations developing and supplying standard consumer products — a procedure may be needed to document how product requirements are determined. This could cover such activities as research of customer needs and expectations, evaluation of competitive products, and market testing. The procedure should also explain how this information is converted into specific product or service requirements.

RECORDS The evidence of compliance may include, as applicable, contract review records, service records, customer feedback records, customer surveys, market testing reports, design input and design validation records, specifications of pertinent legal and regulatory requirements, and so forth.

AUDIT Auditors will focus on verifying that product requirements not directly specified by the customer are also considered and identified. For example, this could be safety, packaging, or regulatory requirements.

In companies that specify their own product requirements, such as in standard consumer products, auditors will be also interested in how information about customer needs, expectations, and preferences is converted into specific product requirements. Auditors will have no specific expectations of how this should be done, but they will want to see that this process is defined and controlled.

7.2.2   Review of of Requirements Related to Product

REQUIREMENT   *Prior to commitment to supply product to customer, review product requirements and resolve any differences or ambiguities.*

IMPLEMENTATION   The method and depth of the review will vary significantly depending on the type of product, extent of company involvement in the origination of specifications, the manner in which the order is received, and the relationship between the supplier and the customer.

The most basic type of review would apply to an order for a catalog product stocked by the supplier. The review would consist of verification that the ordered items are positively identified, that they are in stock, and can be delivered on the requested date.

A more complex review would be carried out where an order from a customer is received as a form, fit, and function specification only, and requires the company to design and manufacture the product. An extreme example would be a contract for design and delivery of a ship or a power plant. Initial site visits, conceptual technical proposals, contract negotiations, and all other types and forms of contact with the customer would be a part of the contract review process. When design is required, many of the contract review activities will overlap with the design input verification activities (refer to Clause 7.3.2).

When a verbal order is received, the order should be confirmed. The customer can be given a written confirmation, or the order can be verbally repeated back to the customer to verify that the customer's requirements have been well understood.

When applicable, the review should also verify that the resolution of any differences to the originally specified requirements is addressed in the contract, especially when the differences involve custom products designed and manufactured to meet customer specification.

The NOTE at the end of this clause considers automated order taking setups, such as sales from an Internet site or a vending machine, where an actual review of each order is not practical. The standard suggests that in these cases the review should instead focus on relevant product information, such as catalogs or advertising material. One might add that in Internet sales there should always be a confirming e-mail sent to the customer.

DOCUMENTATION Although not explicitly required in the standard, there should be a procedure on how to take orders and how to review them as required in this clause. For catalog or standard products, the procedure should require verification of product description, quantity and price; delivery details; any special packaging, storage and delivery requirements; spare parts; and quality records (certificates, test and inspection reports, etc.). The verification can be performed by reviewing customer's previous orders to ensure there are no obvious inconsistencies, by repeating the order back to the customer for confirmation, or any other method that effectively verifies the order. The procedure should also designate personnel responsible for conducting the review and verification (it may be the same person that takes and processes the order), and define what constitutes a record of the review and its result.

Contract review procedure for custom products will not be as specific as above, because it must cover a greater variation in the nature and complexity of orders, but should address the same spectrum of issues.

RECORDS The evidence of compliance consists of contract review records. A simple way to establish a contract review record for catalog or standard product is to initial and/or stamp REVIEWED or ACCEPTED directly on the order. In electronic systems, checkboxes or fields for entering initials of the reviewer could be included in the computerized order entry forms. For more complex reviews, it may be necessary to circulate relevant documents to the affected departments for sign-off. The record can be in any form, including check-marked lists, stamps, sign-offs, minutes of meetings, or copies of internal or external communication.

AUDIT

To assess compliance, auditors will review a sample of contracts and customer purchase orders to verify that the documents were reviewed prior to acceptance. Auditors will also inspect the records of returned products and customer complaints, noting whether there are cases of nonconforming shipments caused by misunderstanding of customer requirements.

REQUIREMENT

Verify the capability and capacity to meet product and customer requirements.

IMPLEMENTATION

Methods for verifying the capability and capacity to meet customer requirements can vary significantly, depending on the type of product and the requirements. They also depend on whether the product is standard or custom, and whether design is involved.

The capacity to ship standard stock items can be simply verified by checking that the ordered items are available. For custom products involving design, the assessment of the capability to meet customer requirements should include, as appropriate, the verification that:

- Specifications can be met;
- Required tolerances are attainable;
- Manufacturing processes are developed and are capable, and that their performance can be recorded using SPC if so required in the contract;
- Required materials and equipment are available;
- There is sufficient manpower capacity;

- Special requirements — quality, packaging, delivery, etc. — can be met;
- Regulatory, environmental and safety requirements are known and can be satisfied; etc.

Verification of the capacity to meet requirements for complex custom products will often involve several departments and may include consultants and subcontractors.

DOCUMENTATION The operational procedure dealing with contract review for standard products should instruct what specific steps must be taken to verify that the ordered products are in stock, or can be manufactured before the requested delivery date; and that special customer requirements, such as customized features, accessories, or special packaging, can be met. In the case of custom products, the procedure would be more general, to cover for a greater variation in the types of products and requirements. Because custom orders usually require special production runs, and often design and subcontracting also, the main focus of the procedure would be to ensure that all relevant functions, such as engineering, production, or purchasing, participate in contract review.

RECORDS The evidence of compliance would be provided by any type of record demonstrating that the ability and capacity to meet contract requirements was verified. For standard products, the record is usually the same as for the general review (see preceding requirement). For complex custom contracts, there may be a sign-off sheet where each concerned department confirms its ability to meet product specifications and other requirements.

AUDIT Auditors will examine a sample of customer purchase orders to verify that a review was conducted prior to acceptance. Customer complaints and returned products records will be examined to assess the effectiveness of the system. Auditors will also compare the requested delivery dates to the actual shipping dates. When there is a pattern of late deliveries, auditors will investigate further to determine whether inadequate communication between sales and other departments is to blame. If so, they may raise a finding against this clause.

REQUIREMENT

Ensure that changes to product or customer requirements are reviewed and are communicated to relevant personnel, and that appropriate documents are amended.

IMPLEMENTATION

The system for processing change orders usually parallels that for accepting new orders. The change orders are matched with the initial orders that they amend, and are reviewed for the adequacy and completeness of stated requirements, and whether there is sufficient capacity to meet the changed or additional requirements.

The main difference is that, while initial orders are fed into the system from one end and are then sequentially processed by different departments, change orders may need to be communicated simultaneously to many departments. It may be necessary to intercept the processing of the initial order in design, production control, production, and/or shipping; withdraw from these locations any documents superseded by the changes; and replace with revised documents.

DOCUMENTATION

The operational procedure for order processing and review should have a special section dealing with change orders. The procedure should explain how to receive and route change orders; designate personnel responsible for their review; instruct in the scope of the review; define what constitutes the record of the review; and instruct how change order requirements are communicated to other concerned functions.

RECORDS

Records demonstrating compliance with this requirement are substantially the same as for the initial contract review (refer to the two previous requirements). In addition, distribution lists of relevant documents, such as revised drawings or specifications, should demonstrate that changed requirements were communicated to all concerned functions.

AUDIT   Auditors will review a sample of change orders and the evidence of associated communication with the customer and within the company. The audit will verify that change orders are being reviewed, that they are formally accepted and authorized before implementation, and that all concerned functions are promptly informed about the changes. A common problem occurs when changes are implemented in design or production before the actual acceptance of the change order by the customer and/or release of revised specifications and drawings.

7.2.3   Customer Communication

REQUIREMENT   *Define and implement arrangements for communicating with customers.*

IMPLEMENTATION   This innocent-sounding clause is nothing less than a requirement to integrate into the quality system such functions as marketing, sales, and customer service, and to define and control all communication with customers.

To implement this requirement, all functions that communicate directly with customers must have defined requirements. In practice, this means procedures and work instructions.

DOCUMENTATION   The quality manual should identify the points of interface and communication with customers, outline corresponding arrangements, assign responsibilities and authorities, and reference applicable procedures.

Where processes for communicating with customers are relatively simple they can be documented in a common procedure addressing all requirements of Clause 7.2. Such procedure could be called *Customer Requirements and Communication*, for example.

Another strategy would be to create separate procedures for each relevant department, such as for marketing, customer service, and sales. Procedures dealing with customer complaints and actions relating to nonconforming (returned) product are also relevant to this clause.

RECORDS

There are no records that need to be established in response to this requirement. The evidence of compliance will be provided by documents defining arrangements for communicating with customers (procedures and work instructions).

AUDIT

Auditors will be looking for procedures, work instructions, checklists, and other such documents defining processes for communicating with customers. This should include providing product and/or service information, handling of inquires and orders, technical support, product servicing requests, customer complaints, other customer feedback, and so forth.

7.3 DESIGN AND DEVELOPMENT

7.3.1 Design and Development Planning

REQUIREMENT

Plan design and development activities, define organizational and technical interfaces, and assign responsibilities and authorities.

IMPLEMENTATION

To satisfy this requirement, every design and development project should:

- Be divided into individual design activities and design phases, to include also design review, verification, and validation that are appropriate to each design phase;
- Have a schedule for the completion of main activities and phases;
- Have assigned qualified personnel with defined responsibilities and authorities; and

- Have defined technical interfaces (communication of information and data) between various internal and external design groups.

Planning shall be updated as the design and development progresses.

For a simple routine design project, all these requirements can be addressed using a design planning and scheduling chart. It would list all design activities and identify for each the assigned personnel or team, the design input, the required output, and the start and completion dates. Such chart would not only satisfy this requirement for design project planning, but also requirements pertaining to design input and output, and design verification. Example of a design planning and scheduling chart is provided in Jack Kanholm's *ISO 9000 Documentation* software.

For large and complex design projects, a more sophisticated project management system will be expected. It would include such elements as critical path scheduling, project organization charts, logs tracking transmittal and receipt of documents and information, schedules for release of drawings and specifications, and procedures for progress and design review meetings.

Responsibilities for specific design functions should be assigned to qualified personnel. When design input comes from different sources, such as various departments or teams, or external organizations, the interrelationship and interfaces between these groups should be clearly defined, understood, and controlled.

DOCUMENTATION Although the standard does not explicitly require a procedure for managing design projects, it is customary to have such a procedure and auditors will expect it. For simple and routine design projects the procedure can be quite specific. It can instruct how to establish the design planning and scheduling chart and assign the responsibility for this activity. When projects are more complex and unpredictable, the procedure should be more flexible. It may only outline the general system for managing design projects, and require that more specific procedures be established for each individual project.

For large projects, with participation of many external consultants, several procedures may be required to establish a comprehensive system for design project management. The relevant elements would be, for example, planning, scheduling, assignment of activities, communication of information and data, and approvals and releases of output documents.

RECORDS
The records and evidence of compliance are provided by the documents established in the course of planning and scheduling design projects. These may be flowcharts, schedules, organizational charts, assignments of responsibilities, memoranda, minutes of meetings, etc.

AUDIT
To verify compliance, auditors will review a number of design project books and/or files to verify that all documents required by procedures are being established and utilized. They will verify that project schedules, activity plans, assignment of personnel, and definition of technical interfaces are consistently established for every design project. Auditors may also ask for evidence that the assigned personnel meet qualification requirements.

7.3.2   Design and Development Inputs

REQUIREMENT
Determine, document and review design input requirements.

IMPLEMENTATION
Design input requirements are the physical, functional, and performance characteristics of the product being designed. Design input must at least include functional and/or performance specification and applicable statutory and regulatory requirements.

Design input is defined by the customer. The customer can be internal or external. An internal customer is usually the marketing or business development department that, based on market research, specifies new product briefs, which are then used as design input. An external customer is either the end user, another company, or another division.

Design input should be specified to the level of detail necessary to permit the design activity to be completed effectively and to provide a consistent basis for design decisions and design verification. It should include the results of a structured assessment of possible hazards associated with the use and/or application of the product and, where relevant, any applicable regulatory requirements.

ISO 9001 requires that the design input be formally documented (even when the customer is internal) and be reviewed by the designers for adequacy and completeness. Any ambiguous or conflicting requirements should be resolved before the design input requirements are used in developing the design. Changes or amendments to the design input should be likewise reviewed and approved.

This requirement for documenting and reviewing design input parallels the requirement for the review of product requirements (contract review) in Clause 7.2.2. In fact, when design input is defined in the technical sections of a contract, the preliminary review of design input will be carried out within the scope of contract review.

DOCUMENTATION The operational procedure governing the control of design input should include instructions on how the design input should be documented; who approves it; what constitutes the record of approval; how to distinguish an approved document from a preliminary document; how the design input is communicated to the design team; and how changes in the design input are documented, approved, and communicated.

RECORDS The records and evidence of compliance are provided by documents defining the design input for current and completed projects, and records of their review and approval.

AUDIT Assessing compliance, auditors will review a number of design project books and files to verify that design input documents are being established and approved in accordance with procedures. Audiotrs will investigate how the applicable statutory and regulatory requirements have been identified, and will verify that the requirements were included in the design input.

Auditors will also test the effectiveness of communicating the design input requirements to design teams or individuals. Audiotrs will ask engineers and consultants about their design input, how it was communicated to them, and how they know that the input they use is authorized. Handling of design changes will be investigated using similar techniques.

7.3.3 Design and Development Outputs

REQUIREMENT *Ensure that design outputs are in a form that enables verification against input requirements, and include all information necessary for product realization and verification.*

IMPLEMENTATION Design output is usually documented in specifications, drawings, bills of materials, parts lists, software, manufacturing specifications and drawings, inspection procedures, service procedures, and other such documents.

All requirements in this clause are reasonable and important but are not readily auditable, at least not by a third-party certification audit. Auditors cannot be expected to have the knowledge and time to independently verify that the design output is complete in all respects required in the standard. For example, how would auditors know that the design output provides all appropriate information for purchasing, or that it completely specifies all characteristics of the product that are essential for its safe and proper use? To make this kind of assessment auditors would have to be experts in the field and have the time to carefully examine all design output documents.

This does not mean that the requirements in this clause can be ignored. They must be documented, implemented, and verified by internal auditing. Internal auditors should have the expertise and time to fully verify compliance.

DOCUMENTATION The operational procedure dealing with design control should contain a section dedicated to design output. The procedure should require that the design output be documented and that the output documents:

- Be in a form that enables verification against design input requirements;

- Provide all necessary information for realization of the product;

- Define product acceptance and release criteria; and

- Specify characteristics that are essential for safe and proper use of the product.

RECORDS The evidence of compliance consists of the design output documents themselves, as well as control plans and associated inspection and testing procedures.

AUDIT Verifying compliance will not be easy, but auditors will ask questions anyway. They will ask how some specific design input requirements have been met and documented, and how was that verified. They will also ask how acceptance criteria were defined and/or referenced, and will review a sample of relevant documents to verify implementation. When acceptance criteria are expressed in terms of samples and workmanship standards, auditors will expect the samples to be approved and be otherwise controlled like other design output documents.

Common problems are lack of tolerances on measurements and other characteristics, undefined surface finishes and other appearance requirements, and incomplete and ambiguous testing requirements.

REQUIREMENT　*Review and approve design outputs before release.*

IMPLEMENTATION　Review of design output documents should not be confused with design verification. The kind of review required in this section is often called engineering inspection. The purpose of the review is to check and coordinate drawings, specifications, and other design output documents, to ensure that they are complete and correct. But this is not verification of the design itself — a faulty design can still be well documented. The review and approval of design output documents should be evidenced by a signature of an authorized person, and the approved documents should be controlled in accordance with Clause 4.2.3, Control of Documents.

DOCUMENTATION　The quality manual should include a policy that all design output documents be reviewed and approved before release, and an operational procedure that explains in detail how this policy is implemented. The procedure should define who is responsible for reviewing the documents and who has the authority to approve them; provide guidelines regarding the scope of the review; instruct how to establish the review records (sign-off on documents, in a log, etc.); and explain how to distinguish approved documents from preliminary and other documents that are not approved for use in production.

RECORDS　The records and evidence of compliance are provided by the review and approval sign-offs in the design output documents or in logs.

AUDIT　Assessing compliance, auditors will look for approval signatures on design output documents (or initials or other identification on electronic documents, such as CAD drawings). In fact, auditors always check for authorizing signatures whenever they see a drawing, specification, or other engineering document. It is a reflex.

7.3.4   Design and Development Review

REQUIREMENT   *At suitable design stages, plan and conduct design reviews.*

IMPLEMENTATION   The purpose of design reviews is to assess and verify the evolving design at various stages. Design reviews should not be confused with design project coordination and management activities, although both can be conducted at the same meeting. Design reviews should consider the adequacy and completeness of the design input; safety and regulatory compliance of the design; requirements for, and results of, the design verification and validation program; production requirements; inspection feasibility; and so forth. The overall objective of design reviews is to assess the effectiveness of the design in meeting the design input requirements.

Design reviews must be planned in advance and be included in the design project schedule. The meetings are conducted by the design team, but should also include representatives of other departments concerned with the design stage being reviewed. Typically, apart from the design team, the marketing, production, and quality assurance departments would be involved in the design reviews at relevant stages.

ISO 9001 does not explicitly state how many, or at which design stages, design reviews must be conducted. The generally accepted interpretation is that even the smallest design project should have at least two design reviews: one following the planning and design input review stage (it may also be combined with design input review), and the other in conjunction with the final approval of the design. Larger projects would have a review following completion of every design phase, or have a regularly scheduled design review — for example, weekly or monthly — depending on the nature and pace of the project.

DOCUMENTATION

There should be an operational procedure defining requirements for and instructing how to conduct design reviews. The procedure should assign responsibility for scheduling design reviews; determine who should participate in the reviews; provide guidelines regarding the scope of the reviews; provide guidelines for establishing the agenda for the reviews; and instruct how to establish the review records (sign-off on documents, meeting minutes, etc.).

RECORDS

The standard explicitly requires that design review records be established and maintained. Usually, these are minutes of design review meetings or reports with their conclusions. The records should document who participated in the review, what aspects of the design were reviewed, and what are the conclusions and recommendations of the review. Other relevant records would be approvals of design output documents, samples, and performance test reports.

AUDIT

Assessing compliance, auditors will examine the design review records from current and completed design projects. Auditors may also follow up on some specific conclusions and recommendations to check that they were implemented.

7.3.5   Design and Development Verification

REQUIREMENT

Verify designs to ensure that design outputs meet the design input requirements.

IMPLEMENTATION

The extent of design verification required depends on the safety, performance, and reliability requirements for the product. Other factors to be considered are the complexity of the design, the existence of published technical standards, the current state of the art, and the similarity with previously proven designs. Also, design verification requirements may sometimes be specified in contracts.

When design reviews are conducted at appropriate stages of design, the reviews may be credited toward satisfying this requirement. Design reviews are part of the verification process. In addition, the standard suggests other possible methods to verify the design, such as performing alternative calculations, comparing the new design with a similar proven design, undertaking tests and demonstrations, and reviewing the design-stage documents before release.

Design comparison may be appropriate when a new application is identified for a proven design, new technology is compared with an existing product, two proven product designs are combined to create a new product, or a new product is substantially equivalent to an existing product.

At the conclusion of each phase of the design cycle, systematic and critical verification of the design output should be conducted and documented to ensure that it meets the design input requirements for this stage.

DOCUMENTATION There should be an operational procedure explaining how design verification is planned, how the plan is documented, what verification methods will be employed, and how the verified design-stage documents are approved for use in the next design stage.

If design review is the most frequently used verification method, this procedure can be combined with the procedure for design reviews. The title of the procedure (or sectional heading) could be, for example, "Design Review and Verification" to quickly establish that it addresses both activities.

RECORDS Design verification must be recorded. The records should identify the design-stage that was verified, the verification methods used, and the person or team that carried out the verification. The verified design-stage documents should be authorized for use and/or release.

AUDIT When assessing compliance, auditors will review a sample of design project files, noting whether feasibility studies, preliminary drawings, calculations, and other design-stage documents have been verified and approved. They will also check that engineers and other design personnel use approved design-stage input documents in their current work. Any comparison of existing products used for verification purposes may also be reviewed.

7.3.6   Design and Development Validation

REQUIREMENT   *Validate designs to ensure that resulting product is capable of meeting requirements for specified application or intended use.*

IMPLEMENTATION   Validation of design is usually performed with a prototype of the product by testing it under real or simulated conditions. The objective of design validation is to confirm that the design satisfies the expected user needs and/or requirements with regard to performance, durability, reliability, serviceability, safety, and other such characteristics.

Design validation should be planned and coordinated with other design verification activities. The plan should prescribe a specific testing procedure for each anticipated mode of use and the tested characteristic.

Upon completion of the validation process, the final design configuration must be documented and manufacturing specifications established prior to release to production.

DOCUMENTATION   The operational procedure dealing with design control should have a section dedicated to design validation and/or prototype testing. The procedure should assign responsibility for coordinating the validation activity, require establishment of detailed testing procedures, and define who should evaluate and approve the test results and how.

RECORDS   In addition to the operational procedure, there may also be a need for specific testing instructions for each anticipated mode of use and tested characteristic. The instructions should explain the setup, testing parameters, data collection and analysis, and reporting.

Results and conclusions of design validation testing must be recorded. The format and content of prototype testing reports should be defined in specific testing procedures (instructions).

AUDIT When assessing compliance, auditors will review the design validation and testing procedures, test results and reports. The areas used for testing will also be inspected to review setups and verify that only calibrated measuring instruments are used. Auditors will specifically ask for the evidence that test results are evaluated against specified requirements (design input).

7.3.7   Control of Design and Development Changes

REQUIREMENT *Identify and document design changes and review, verify, and validate changes before implementation.*

IMPLEMENTATION Identification of required or desired design changes may come from many different sources inside and outside the company. The system for processing design changes should define how internal departments, customers, and users should communicate their requests for design changes.

Design changes may be necessary as a result of experience in use, changes in market requirements, changes of regulatory requirements, material or process changes, desire to improve manufacturability, and many other such factors. Requests for changes must first be evaluated whether the requested change should be implemented or not.

Once a request for change is accepted, the remaining activities — implementation of the change and verification and validation of the changed design — should basically follow the same procedures that apply to original designs.

The standard also requires a review of the effect of the changes on the overall design and on products already delivered.

DOCUMENTATION The operational procedure dealing with design changes should provide forms or other means for identifying and documenting design changes; provide guidelines for evaluating change requests; and explain how design changes are to be implemented, verified, and recorded.

RECORDS The records and evidence of compliance consist of all documents established in the course of initiating and implementing design changes. Forms used for initiating and documenting design changes are often referred to as ECRs (Engineering Change Requests) or ECNs (Engineering Change Notices).

Such forms can be designed specifically to address particular requirements of this clause. For example, the form could include a check box for marking that the change was reviewed for impact on the overall design and on product already shipped. An example of an ECR form is provided in Jack Kanholm's *ISO 9001 Documentation* software.

AUDIT When assessing compliance, auditors will review change order files and engineering change requests (ECRs or ECNs), noting whether they are established and processed in conformance with procedures. Auditors will compare approval and implementation dates to verify that changes are not implemented prior to formal customer or other authorized approval.

7.4 PURCHASING

Requirements of this section apply to purchased products that are intended for incorporation into the final product, and procured services that may affect product quality. Purchased products and services could include:

- Raw materials;
- Components or subassemblies manufactured by others, including standard items, components

manufactured to the company's specifications, and items manufactured using equipment owned by, and/or materials provided by, the company; and

■ Services that may affect product quality, e.g., consulting, calibration, testing, delivery, installation, servicing, and manufacturing equipment maintenance; and in food processing or medical device industry pest control, cleaning, environmental monitoring, and laundry.

7.4.1   Purchasing Process

REQUIREMENT *Evaluate suppliers, monitor their quality performance, and maintain records of their quality capabilities and performance.*

IMPLEMENTATION All subcontractors and suppliers to which this clause applies must be evaluated to determine their ability to meet requirements. The scope and depth of the evaluation will depend on how critical and complex the products to be supplied are, and on what is already known about the supplier.

The scope could include:

■ On-site assessment and evaluation of a subcontractor's resources and quality system;

■ Existing approvals or third-party certifications of the subcontractor's quality system;

■ References from other customers or users;

■ Evaluation of product samples;

■ Experience with similar product;

■ Experience with the subcontractor; or

■ Test results from the subcontractor, including certificates of conformance and analysis.

The company should be able to demonstrate that the assessment system provides:

- Formal consideration of the extent of assessment required;
- Selection based on a sufficiently structured appraisal appropriate to the product or service procured;
- Periodic reassessment of performance; and
- A quality system standard to be applied and methods of verification.

All subcontractors must be continuously monitored with regard to their quality performance. Quality problems should be recorded and brought to the attention of the subcontractors. Subcontractors should be asked to propose and implement corrective actions to address their problems. When appropriate, the monitoring system should also include quality system audits, process capability verifications, and source inspections.

The system for prequalifying and monitoring subcontractors requires collecting and analyzing documents and records that provide information about the subcontractors' capabilities and performance. These can be references, process capability and audit reports, product nonconformity records, corrective action requests, and so forth. The documents should be properly organized and maintained, usually by having a separate quality record file for each subcontractor. The subcontractor quality records should be reviewed regularly, and the conclusions utilized for making decisions regarding their approval status.

DOCUMENTATION The operational procedure for evaluation, approval, and monitoring of subcontractors should assign the responsibility for conducting the evaluations and provide guidelines for determining their scope; outline the elements and scope of the system for monitoring subcontractors' quality performance; and define how the quality assurance and purchasing departments should cooperate and interface in operating the system. If subcontractors are regularly audited, there should also be a procedure instructing how to initiate, conduct, and report subcontractor quality system audits, including audit checklists (the procedure can be combined with the internal audit procedures).

The system for collecting and analyzing subcontractor quality records should be also documented in a procedure. The procedure should explain what kinds of records are collected, who reviews the records and how often, and how the subcontractor approval status is recorded and communicated to other concerned functions.

RECORDS The evidence of compliance consists of the subcontractor quality record files, which contain records of subcontractors' quality capabilities and performance histories. There should also be evidence that the records are regularly reviewed and the information is used in selecting subcontractors.

AUDIT Auditors will verify that all relevant subcontractors and suppliers are prequalified before they receive purchasing contracts, and that their quality performance is being regularly monitored. Auditors will also review the content of the subcontractor quality record files, verifying that the files are maintained, that identified quality problems are communicated back to the subcontractors, and that subcontractors implement corrective actions to address the problems.

REQUIREMENT *Maintain a list of approved suppliers and subcontractors.*

IMPLEMENTATION All functions involved with specifying, requisitioning, and purchasing materials and products should have current information with regard to approval status of subcontractors. This is usually achieved by maintaining and distributing an approved subcontractor list. The list can be maintained on computer and be distributed online, or be printed out. The list must be a controlled document.

DOCUMENTATION Purchasing procedure should assign the responsibility for establishing and maintaining the approved subcontractor list, specify how often the list should be updated, and explain who should use the list and how.

RECORDS Records demonstrating compliance with this requirement are the approved subcontractor list, subcontractor qualification records, and, when required, records evidencing customer approval of subcontractors.

AUDIT To assess compliance, auditors will ask for the approved subcontractor list and will verify that the list is updated regularly and is available to personnel involved with the purchasing.

NOTE: ISO 9001 does not explicitly require that there be a list of approved subcontractors. However, a list is the most common way to communicate internally which subcontractors are acceptable. In a very small organization, or where there are just a few subcontractors, the list may not be necessary as long as all personnel involved in purchasing have access to the actual quality records of acceptable subcontractors.

7.4.2   Purchasing Information

REQUIREMENT *Precisely describe the product to be purchased, including where appropriate requirements for approvals, qualifications, and quality management system.*

IMPLEMENTATION Description of products to be purchased should be as specific and complete as possible, to include part or model numbers for catalog products and revision level of drawings or specifications for custom products.

Where applicable, purchasing documents should specify requirements for prior approval of product samples, procedures, processes or equipment; requirements for qualification of personnel; requirements for product inspection or testing reports, SPC charts, or other evidence of product conformity; and requirements for quality management system (for example, ISO 9001 registration).

The standard also requires that the organization shall ensure the adequacy of specified purchase requirements prior to communicating them to the supplier. The most common way to satisfy this requirement is by reviewing purchasing documents to verify that the information is accurate and complete. However, a review is not explicitly mentioned (it was in the earlier editions of the standard) and thus other appropriate methods to ensure the adequacy can be used instead. Examples include a checklist for establishing purchase orders, or purchasing specification sheets listing requirements that must be included in purchase orders for particular products.

The review of purchasing documents (if such review is carried out) should ensure that the subcontractor is approved; the products are adequately defined; all relevant quality requirements are stated; possible regulatory issues are addressed; and packaging, labeling and delivery requirements, including requested delivery dates, are clearly specified. The review should be recorded, which can simply be an approval signature.

DOCUMENTATION The procedure for establishing purchasing documents should assign the responsibility and authority for review and approval of purchasing documents, and outline the scope of the review. It should also specify what constitutes the record of review and how to distinguish approved documents. In addition, or instead of requiring review and approval, the procedure should provide a checklist of product features and characteristics that may be relevant when describing products in purchasing documents, and a checklist of common requirements, such as certificates of conformance, material certificates, packaging and delivery requirements, etc. (This kind of information may also be included in product specifications.)

RECORDS Usually, the only records and evidence of implementation are the approval signatures on purchasing documents, unless the system also requires establishment of other records, such as review checklists, for example.

AUDIT

Assessing compliance, auditors will review a sample of purchase orders, checking how products are described and if the documents are approved. Auditors may also interview personnel who prepare purchasing documents and who review the documents, to verify that the personnel know and use the procedures relevant to these activities. Common omissions in purchase orders are imprecise description of ordered products, lack of revision level identification for drawings, and lack of requests for material certificates, testing reports, or traceability records.

NOTE: Review and approval of purchasing documents is not explicitly required in the standard. The requirement is for ensuring the adequacy of the documents, and a review is just one way, albeit the most popular way, of satisfying this requirement.

7.4.3 Verification of Purchased Products

REQUIREMENT

Inspect or otherwise verify purchased product to ensure that it meets specified purchase requirements.

IMPLEMENTATION

Verification of purchased products is mandatory, but it does not always need to be a receiving inspection. When there is credible evidence that effective controls were employed during the products' manufacture and that the products have been inspected before dispatch, the receiving inspection can be limited to the identification of the products, review of records and certificates supplied with the products (for example, material certificates or SPC records), and verification that the products and/or their packaging have not been damaged during transportation.

The decision regarding how much and what kind of receiving inspection should be required for a given product must be based on the following principle: The product characteristics and aspects that are left out of the receiving inspection can only be those that have already been verified by the supplier or subcontractor.

Reduction of the scope of receiving inspection should be justified by appropriate quality records provided by the subcontractor. These can be final inspection reports, certificates of conformance, or inspection stamps on products. In addition, there should also be evidence that the subcontractor operates an effective quality management system. If such quality records are not available, all critical aspects of received products should be physically inspected.

To prevent uninspected or nonconforming products from being used or processed, the physical arrangement of receiving areas should be adapted to minimize intermingling of products having different inspection status. There should be dedicated locations for products awaiting inspection, and for each stage of the inspection process.

Nonconforming products should be segregated. Products, the conformance of which cannot be determined because of the lack of certificates or other records, should be considered nonconforming, at least temporarily. In addition to segregation, products with different inspection status should be appropriately labeled (see Clause 7.5.3).

DOCUMENTATION The operational procedure dealing with verification of purchased product (receiving inspections) should provide policy guidelines, assign the authority for determining how much and what kind of receiving inspection will be applied to purchased products, and how this determination is to be documented and communicated (control plans, inspection procedures, etc.). The procedure should also explain the entire system for receiving products, including checking shipments against purchase orders, reviewing and filing supplied quality records, inspecting the received products, establishing inspection records, releasing products for urgent production purposes, and labeling products with their inspection status identification. Work instructions may be required for carrying out specific inspections and tests.

RECORDS

The records and evidence of compliance consist of receiving inspection records and other records demonstrating conformity of purchased products. Also relevant are arrangements for identifying inspection status of product, such as labels, tags, markings or designated storage locations.

AUDIT

To assess compliance, auditors will review the receiving inspection records and verify that the records are established in accordance with governing procedures. Audiotrs may pick a sample of closed-out purchase orders and ask for corresponding receiving records, or pick a couple of received products and start from there. Auditors will also verify that products with different inspection status are adequately segregated and are appropriately labeled. If possible, auditors will want to witness some inspections, verifying that inspectors are qualified, that they use calibrated measuring equipment, and that inspection procedures are available and are used.

7.5   PRODUCTION AND SERVICE PROVISION

7.5.1   Control of Production and Service Provision

REQUIREMENT

Ensure that production and service provision are carried out under controlled conditions.

IMPLEMENTATION

Clause 7.5.1 includes a list of specific conditions and aspects that need to be controlled in production. It can be summarized as follows:

a) Availability of information defining the product;

b) Availability of work instructions;

c) The use of suitable equipment;

d) Availability of monitoring and measuring devices;

e) The implementation of process and product inspection and testing; and

f) The implementation of release, delivery and post-delivery activities.

None of the items in the list are unique to this clause. All are addressed more specifically in other places in the standard. This clause is just a consolidation and summary. Specifically, availability of product information is covered under clauses dealing with documentation (4.2) and design output (7.3.3); work instructions are discussed in the next requirement under this clause (7.5.1); use of suitable equipment is addressed in clauses dealing with planning of realization processes (7.1) and infrastructure (6.3); measuring devices will be addressed under the clause for control of measuring equipment (7.6); inspection, testing and product release will be covered in the clause dealing with monitoring and measuring of product (8.2.4); and delivery activities in the clause for preservation of product (7.5.5).

DOCUMENTATION The general commitment to establish and maintain controlled conditions for production and service provision should be documented in the quality manual. At this level, the manual should name the six areas of control corresponding to items (a) through (f); commit to establish and maintain adequate controls in those areas; and reference procedures defining the specific controls.

RECORDS The records and evidence of compliance are discussed under other clauses where corresponding requirements are stated more specifically.

AUDIT In itself, this clause is not readily auditable, because it lacks any specifics requirements against which a finding could be clearly identified. But it does not matter, because all its elements can be enforced under other clauses where corresponding requirements are stated more specifically.

REQUIREMENT   *Provide personnel with work instructions and define workmanship criteria.*

IMPLEMENTATION   Work instructions and workmanship criteria may be in the form of manuals, procedures, data sheets, posted signs, photographs, product and material samples, and other such documents and physical samples. They instruct how to operate a process or carry out a task, or set a standard for the level of workmanship. Examples include how to change tooling; feed, fasten, or handle materials; carry out an inspection or test; calibrate a measuring instrument; establish a record; and so forth. Work instructions are usually written internally by the company, but may also be published by others, such as equipment operating instructions published by its manufacturer.

The need for work instructions for a given process should be determined based on the importance and complexity of the process, operator qualifications, history of quality problems with the process, and other such relevant considerations. The standard does not set any specific criteria for determining whether work instructions will be required or not. It only states that the documentation must be sufficient to ensure effective control of processes.

In practice, work instructions will always be expected for setups where there are numerical parameters, such as temperature or speed, to be set or maintained; for inspections, tests, and calibrations; and for operating equipment and processes that require following a particular sequence or method.

Workmanship standards should be provided whenever a significant variation in a product characteristic can result from differences in work skills and methods of individual operators. Typically, this applies to manual processes that affect appearance. Workmanship standards may be samples, photographs, patterns and fixtures, written procedures, or in any other form.

Work instructions must be issued as controlled documents. Workmanship standards must be also controlled like documents, even when they are samples, photographs, or fixtures. They must be identified to the product, including revision level, and be authorized for use.

DOCUMENTATION An operational procedure for work instructions and workmanship standards is not required. But many companies would want to have such a procedure. If established, the procedure would provide guidelines for determining when work instructions and standards are needed, and specify who is authorized to issue these instructions. Where these things are relatively simple they may be documented directly in the quality manual, without the need for a procedure.

RECORDS The records and evidence of compliance are the work instructions and workmanship standards themselves.

AUDIT Auditors will ask about the criteria for deciding whether work instructions and workmanship standards are needed, and who makes these decisions. They will review a sample of operations and processes to verify that proper instructions are available and are used when applicable. Where there are no work instructions, auditors may want to evaluate operator qualifications and quality performance of the process to determine whether the lack of written instructions is justifiable. Likewise, auditors will expect workmanship standards where manual operations may cause excessive variations in appearance or other product characteristics. Auditors will also verify that work instructions and workmanship standards are controlled in accordance with requirements of Clause 4.2.3, Control of Documents.

7.5.2   Validation of Processes for Production and Service Provision

REQUIREMENT *Validate processes for production and service provision where the resulting output cannot be verified by subsequent inspection.*

IMPLEMENTATION These processes are often called special processes. Typical examples are joining of materials by welding, soldering, splicing, or gluing; molding and casting of metals, plastics, or cements; coatings with metals, epoxies, paints, plastic, and insulation materials; heat, radiation, or chemical treatment of materials; sterilization and disinfecting; or provision of services where deficiencies become apparent only after the service has been delivered, for example, teaching, live entertainment, or provision of medical care.

The first step in implementing this requirement is to review all production processes and identify those that need to be validated to comply with this clause.

Validation must be carried out following a specified method or procedure and with reference to defined criteria for approval of the process. When applicable, approval of equipment and qualification of personnel shall be included in the criteria. Special processes should be revalidated, either periodically or at certain events, such as tool change, for example.

DOCUMENTATION With regard to documentation, this requirement should be addressed on at least two levels: in the quality manual, with a commitment to validate all special processes; and in work instructions, with detailed validation protocols (methods). An operational procedure is not required, and it would not add much value in most organizations. The general framework for validating and controlling special processes can be usually documented in the quality manual alone. However, if there already is a general procedure for process control, it should be made complete to also address special processes. In any event, the backbone of the documentation are specific validation protocols for all relevant processes. The requirements for revalidation must also be documented.

RECORDS Validation should be carefully recorded. The record should include validation results and description of all relevant factors, such as setup, materials, equipment, qualification of personnel, environmental conditions, etc.

AUDIT when assessing compliance, auditors will first want to know how special processes were identified and by whom; and how was it determined which processes will be validated, which method will be used, and what the approval criteria will be. Next, auditors will select a number of special processes to be examined in more detail and will review the corresponding validation protocols and reports. They will pay attention to whether the actual operational conditions and factors are the same as were used for validation. A common problem is the lack of clearly defined revalidation requirements.

7.5.3   Identification and Traceability

REQUIREMENT *Where appropriate, identify product throughout production and service provision.*

IMPLEMENTATION Tangible products are usually identified by part numbers or, when generic materials are involved, by their trade names. Service products may be identified by title, customer name, or just a descriptive phrase. The identification numbers and names should be the same as those used in drawings, bills of materials, purchase orders, work orders, and other documentation defining the products and methods of production.

Materials and components are normally identified using markings, tags, or labels applied directly to the products or to their packaging or containers. Sub-assemblies, products moving through production processes, as well as many service products can be identified by work orders or travellers (also called shop tickets, flow tags, routing cards, etc.) that are kept together with the products. Identification of final products should be defined in product drawings, specifications, or artwork for labels or packaging.

Product identification should be maintained throughout all stages of receiving, storage, production, and delivery. Products can be left unidentified only when their identity is inherently obvious.

DOCUMENTATION Although an operational procedure for product identification is not required, it will often be necessary, especially where there is a system for generating and managing part numbers. Such a procedure would explain how part numbers are generated and who is responsible for their assignment; how the assignment of part numbers is recorded; and what means are used for identifying different categories of products, and who is responsible for applying the identification. The procedure should also instruct all personnel to protect and maintain the markings, tags, and labels that identify products.

Work instructions may be required when the identification system is complex and needs to be explained in detail, beyond what can be done in an operational procedure. Also, complex methods for product marking may require written instructions.

RECORDS The records and evidence of compliance consist of bills of materials, parts lists, catalogs, and other documentation and records of assigned part numbers; and the tags, labels, and markings that physically identify products.

AUDIT Assessing compliance, auditors will review the system of assigning, documenting, and recording part numbers, paying special attention to parts lists. The lists must be established and maintained as controlled documents in conformance with the requirements of

Clause 4.2.3. On the implementation level, auditors will verify that all materials, components, and products are identified at all stages of production.

REQUIREMENT

Where required, uniquely identify products and maintain records to ensure traceability.

IMPLEMENTATION

ISO 9001 does not require traceability. However, where a traceability system exists, it must be documented, implemented, and controlled as would any other element of the quality system.

Traceability can be required by a customer or a regulatory agency, or it can be implemented voluntarily to facilitate fault diagnosis in defective products. In some cases traceability may not be explicitly required but must be implemented to demonstrate that product meets specified requirements. For example, if extreme strength requirements are specified, and materials must be tested and certified to ascertain their suitability, use of these materials in a product must be recorded so that the material testing certificates can be used to provide the evidence that the product meets the specified strength requirements. In fact, whenever tested and certified materials are used, traceability is an implied requirement.

Traceability systems are normally based on identifying products with batch or serial numbers, or date and time of production, and recording the raw materials, components, and processes used in their manufacture. Where required, traceability may also have to include distribution and end users (shipping records).

Whether the traceability system is specified by external requirements or is implemented voluntarily, its scope and extent must be precisely defined and documented in procedures or product documentation.

DOCUMENTATION

Traceability should be documented on two levels: product level and system level. On the product level there should be a traceability plan for each product type. It should clearly specify:

- Which materials, components, operations, and processes must be traceable;

- What information should be recorded; and

- How traceability records should be established, and how long they must be maintained.

Traceability requirements can be defined in different documents, such as drawings, specifications, procedures, work orders, etc.

On the system level, there should be an operational procedure explaining how traceability plans are established, issued and used, to include:

- How to assign serial numbers or other unique identification, and who is responsible for doing it;

- How to establish and correlate traceability records;

- What measures should be employed to safeguard against loss of traceability; and

- What should be done when traceability is lost at any stage.

Work instructions may be required when the traceability system is complex and needs to be explained in detail, beyond what can be done in an operational procedure or by referencing regulations, standards, or customer documents. Also, complex methods for product marking may require written instructions.

RECORDS

The records and evidence of compliance consist of traceability plans, serial batch number records, and traceability records. Markings, tags, labels, and parts lists used for unique identification of products and their components are also part of the evidence.

AUDIT

When assessing compliance, auditors will review the traceability plans and verify that they are authorized and available in receiving, storage, production, and other relevant areas. Audiotrs will also review the traceability records, paying special attention to the completeness and conformity of the records with traceability plans.

On the implementation level, auditors will verify that traceable materials and components are properly identified, and will assess whether measures employed to safeguard against loss of traceability are fully implemented and effective. They will also want to test the traceability system by tracking back all relevant records to a randomly selected product.

REQUIREMENT   *Identify product status with respect to measuring and monitoring requirements (inspection and test status).*

IMPLEMENTATION   The result of every inspection should be evidenced by appropriate identification of the inspected product. It is not sufficient to identify only failed products. Passed products also must be positively identified.

Methods for identifying inspection status can include marking, labeling, and tagging products or the containers and packaging in which they are held; inspection records, such as sign-off in production work orders or other documents that travel with the products; and physical location (segregation) of products with different inspection status. Physical location is only acceptable as a valid inspection status identification method when specific dedicated areas are used and these areas are identified — by posted signs, for example. Physical location of products is also acceptable when the production flow transfer is automated, i.e., it is not possible to introduce or remove products in between processing steps and operations. Whenever possible, in addition to labeling or marking, nonconforming products should be also segregated.

DOCUMENTATION   Although the standard does not require an operational procedure, there are things that need to be documented. Specifically, there is a need to define which identification measures are to be used for different types of products and various production stages, and who has the authority for making these decisions. There should also be instructions for all personnel to safeguard and maintain the applied identification. There are many possible ways this could be documented. It could be just a section in the quality manual; an item at the end of particular inspection and testing instructions; a section in the general product identification procedure; or a self-contained, dedicated procedure.

RECORDS No records are required. The evidence of implementation are the labels, tags, or other means of identification that are applied to products to indicate their inspection status.

AUDIT Assessing compliance, auditors will verify that all products at all stages are properly identified as to their inspection status. A common problem is loss of the receiving inspection status identification when materials or components are transferred from material storage to production areas. This does not need to be a finding if there are other implemented measures for ensuring that only authorized products can be transferred to production.

7.5.4   Customer Property

REQUIREMENT *Identify, verify, protect, and safeguard customer property and report back to customers when their property is lost, damaged, or found to be unsuitable for use.*

IMPLEMENTATION This section applies to materials, components, and equipment supplied by customers for incorporation into the final product; and to equipment used for related activities, for example, production tooling, special handling equipment, special inspection gauges and fixtures, and reusable shipping containers. It also applies to customer's intellectual property, i.e., documents and information. When a company does not receive from its customers any products, equipment, or information, this section does not apply and it can be excluded from the scope of the quality system requirements (refer to Clause 1.2).

The responsibility for suitability and conformity of customer-supplied product lies with the customer. However, the company should not knowingly incorporate nonconforming parts into the products or service supplied to the purchaser.

The system for verification, storage, and protection of customer supplied products can be exactly the same as, or be integrated with, the corresponding system for verification, storage, and protection of purchased products. The system must also ensure compliance with any additional special requirements specified in a contract. There is an additional requirement to notify customers in the event of damage or loss of their products.

DOCUMENTATION If this clause applies, the corresponding section in the quality manual can just refer to other sections and operational procedures that deal with the verification, identification, storage, and protection of purchased product. It must also include a commitment to notify customers in the event of damage or loss of their products. While a dedicated operational procedure is not required, it could be relevant in companies where there are important and complex issues related to customer-supplied products.

RECORDS The records and evidence of compliance are of the same type as those that apply to verification, storage, and handling of purchased products and company-owned equipment. In addition, there may also be reports informing customers of unsuitability, damage, or loss of their products.

AUDIT Auditors will verify general implementation of this requirement as they would do for purchased products. In addition they will ask if there are any special contractual requirements with respect to verification, identification, storage, or handling of customer supplied products, and will verify implementation of such requirements. This could be, for example, a requirement for segregation and special marking of customer-supplied product.

7.5.5   Preservation of Product

Although this clause has only two sentences, it covers quite a number of activities. Specifically: product handling, packaging, storage, protection, and delivery. The old edition of the standard had six separate subclauses to cover the same topics.

Some of the six requirements discussed below may go beyond what is explicitly stated in the standard. But they all reflect established expectations of how these activities should be controlled. For example, while the standard does not explicitly require designated storage areas, it is an established practice in quality management systems to designate specific locations for storage of particular products, or products with different inspection or release status.

REQUIREMENT   *Use appropriate handling methods and equipment to prevent product damage and deterioration.*

IMPLEMENTATION   In most companies, product handling is quite routine. Products are held in various types of containers, tanks, and on pallets, and are transported around production and storage areas using carts, forklift trucks, and cranes. If handling operations are as basic as these, the only issues are selection of appropriate handling equipment; maintenance of the equipment; and, for cranes and forklift trucks, training of equipment operators.

When special handling techniques are necessary — such as the use of gloves, electrostatic mats, double bagging, etc. — the techniques should be explained in work instructions, and/or personnel should be trained in their use.

DOCUMENTATION There is normally no need for an operational procedure for product handling. The general framework can be outlined in the quality manual, and particular handling techniques can be documented in work instructions. If a procedure is established it could also address protection of product (refer to the fifth requirement under this clause). Whether in a procedure or in the quality manual, the documentation should assign the authority and responsibility for selecting and maintaining suitable product handling equipment; define requirements for qualifications and training of equipment operators; and, when applicable, reference work instructions for particular handling techniques.

RECORDS Product handling does not usually require establishment of any records. However, documents such as equipment certificates (especially cranes) and equipment operator training records are relevant for demonstrating compliance.

AUDIT When assessing compliance, auditors will observe and note if product handling equipment is appropriate and is well maintained, if personnel follow work instructions when using special handling techniques, and if there are any signs of products being damaged or at risk because of inappropriate handling. When relevant, auditors will also review equipment certificates and operator training records.

REQUIREMENT *Specify requirements for packaging and labeling, and control these processes.*

IMPLEMENTATION The packaging and labeling should be formally defined in drawings, specifications, or standards. Packaging specifications should be issued and controlled in the same manner as product documentation. When packaging must meet certain performance criteria — such as strength, watertightness or airtightness, protection from bacteriological contamination, etc. — the packaging should be subjected to the same design, design verification, and process control procedures as apply to products.

Packaging should protect product from unacceptable vibrations, shocks, and other transportation hazards. For example, the suitability of the packaging may be demonstrated by journey hazard trials designed to simulate the abuses the package will encounter during routine methods of transit and storage.

Packaging artwork, markings and labeling that include product identification, warning notices, and instructions for use must be specified, and the documents must be controlled in accordance with the general document control requirements. The system for control of shipping packaging and marking should provide for communication and implementation of special customer or shipper requirements.

DOCUMENTATION Although not required in the standard, it is customary to have an operational procedure for packaging and labeling activities. This is especially relevant when packaging and labeling are organized into a department and there is a dedicated function responsible for these activities. The operational procedure should designate the function responsible for specification of packaging and labeling (can be separate); define how special packaging and labeling requirements are to be communicated; and, where special packaging techniques or processes are used, reference the relevant work instructions.

RECORDS The records and evidence of compliance consist of the packaging drawings and specifications, and possibly work instructions for operating packaging processes.

AUDIT When assessing compliance, auditors will check if packaging is formally defined, and will verify that the actual packaging is the same as specified. When packaging requires special processes or techniques, auditors will assess the packaging operations against the same requirements that apply to production.

REQUIREMENT　　*Provide designated and controlled storage areas.*

IMPLEMENTATION　　The requirements of this clause apply to all locations where products are held awaiting use or delivery. They include staging locations in receiving areas, storage locations for purchased materials and components, locations in production areas where products are temporarily held awaiting inspection or the next processing stage, storage locations for manufactured parts and subassemblies, and finished product stocks.

A storage area is designated when it is contained and segregated from other adjacent areas, and is exclusively dedicated and authorized for storage of particular kinds of products. Storage areas do not always need to be separate rooms or be enclosed by a fence. A dedicated rack of shelves or a yellow line on the floor will, in most cases, provide sufficient segregation. When different kinds of products are stored in the same general storage area, each should have its designated location within the area.

Any raw materials, subassemblies, or products that have been rejected or returned by customers should be segregated or, better, placed in a quarantine area to prevent confusion with other materials. When product safety is an issue, access to such areas should be restricted to authorized personnel.

Designation and authorization of storage areas should be identified by posted signs and be documented in a layout plan or a procedure.

DOCUMENTATION　　In most smaller companies there is no need for an operational procedure to manage storage areas. The general framework can be outlined in the quality manual and designation of specific areas can be defined in a layout plan. A procedure would usually be established only where there are special departments, units, or functions dedicated to operating storage areas.

Whether in a procedure or the quality manual, the documentation should include or reference a plan or list designating specific locations for storing particular kinds of product, and define the function responsible for assignment and management of storage areas. There should also be a policy stating that all storage areas must be designated, segregated, and identified by posted signs, and that storage of any products outside of designated storage areas is strictly prohibited. There may also be a need for work instructions, for example, on how to receive or release product from stockrooms, or how to operate the inventory management system.

RECORDS

The records and evidence of compliance consist of layout plans and posted signs that identify the designated specific areas for storage of particular kinds of products.

AUDIT

Assessing compliance, auditors will observe and note if all storage areas are clearly identified and segregated, if they contain only the kinds of products for which they are designated, and if the storage areas are properly organized and maintained. Where applicable, the quarantine areas will be reviewed to assess whether the release and distribution of items to and from those areas is conducted in accordance with defined procedures. Auditors will also look out for and investigate products that are stored or held outside of the designated areas.

REQUIREMENT

Control product with limited shelf life and requiring special storage conditions.

IMPLEMENTATION

Although ISO 9001 does not explicitly require any such controls, auditors will always examine the arrangements for controlling product with limited shelf life and requiring special storage conditions.

Products having a limited shelf life should be expiration dated, and should be issued in rotation according to a documented instruction or schedule. Conditions must be controlled for products that must be stored under specified environmental conditions, such as temperature, humidity or light. There should also be a record demonstrating that the specified storage conditions were continuously maintained, or other arrangements for safeguarding and monitoring the conditions.

DOCUMENTATION There is usually no need for a procedure to address this requirement. In most companies it would be sufficient to generally define in the quality manual how shelf life and environmental conditions are controlled, and to document the actual requirements and controls in product specifications and work instructions. But this is not to say that a procedure is never appropriate. It could be useful in companies that operate refrigerated warehouses, for example. The documentation should define how information about environmental limits is communicated to those responsible for operating storage areas, prescribe or reference specific control methods, and define the requirements for records.

RECORDS The evidence of compliance are expiration dating on the product, and records of environmental conditions, such as temperature or humidity charts. Records of environmental conditions or alarms will only be expected where public safety is an issue. Examples are foods, drugs, and volatile or toxic chemicals.

AUDIT Auditors will walk through storage areas to identify product requiring special storage conditions or having limited shelf life, and will verify that these requirements are met. The most common issues are temporary or transitional storage that does not meet requirements; instruments for monitoring environmental conditions not being calibrated; and lack of any record demonstrating that the required conditions were maintained at all times and that the product was not compromised (required only where public safety may be a factor).

REQUIREMENT   *Protect product during internal processing and storage.*

IMPLEMENTATION   The issues in this requirement are quite similar to
those already discusses for product handling. In most
companies, no special protection or preservation techniques are used. Products are simply protected
against adverse atmospheric conditions and contamination. In most situations, keeping products in
dry and clean storage areas is sufficient. However,
when special preservation methods and techniques
are used, such as specially engineered protective
packaging, application of protective coating on
exposed parts, or maintenance of specified temperature or humidity, the methods should be documented in specifications and work instructions.

DOCUMENTATION   There is normally no need for an operational procedure for product protection and preservation. The
general framework can be outlined in the quality
manual, and particular preservation techniques can
be documented in work instructions. If there is
already a procedure for product handling, it can be
extended to address protection and preservation (refer
to the first requirement under this clause). The procedure (or manual) should assign the responsibility
for developing and implementing suitable product
preservation methods; explain the basic requirements
(dry and clean storage, use of protective packaging,
etc.); and, when applicable, reference specifications
and work instructions for particular preservation
methods.

RECORDS   Product preservation activities usually do not require
establishment of any records. However, when temperature, humidity, or other environmental conditions must be controlled, there should be records to
evidence that the environment is maintained within
specified tolerances.

AUDIT   Assessing compliance, auditors will observe and note
if products are adequately protected; if personnel fol-

low work instructions when applying special preservation methods and techniques; and if there are any signs of products deteriorating, or being at risk, due to inadequate protection or preservation.

REQUIREMENT   *Protect product during delivery.*

IMPLEMENTATION   If delivery is never specified in contracts, this requirement does not apply. If delivery is specified, but is always subcontracted, this requirement should be complied with by exercising the same kind of subcontractor qualification and monitoring controls that apply for purchasing of materials and components (refer to Clause 7.4).

Companies that themselves provide the service of delivering their products must develop methods and techniques to protect the products during delivery. The issues to be addressed are loading techniques, stacking heights, fastening of loads, protection against the elements, and so forth. When special protection techniques are used (for example, control of temperature, or engineered fastening of heavy loads), these should be documented in specifications or procedures.

DOCUMENTATION   When delivery is not relevant or is always subcontracted, there is no need for operational procedure. It is sufficient to state in the quality manual that shippers are controlled in accordance with the same procedures that apply to subcontractors. When delivery is part of the operation, it should be regulated by a procedure. The procedure should assign the responsibility for developing and implementing suitable methods for protecting products during delivery; explain the basic methods (stacking, fastening, protection against the elements, etc.); and, when applicable, reference the specifications and work instructions for special methods.

RECORDS   There are normally no records of product protection during delivery, unless temperature or humidity control records are kept when applicable.

AUDIT   When assessing compliance, auditors will check if the subcontracted shippers are approved, and if their quality performance is monitored. Auditors may also want to observe the loading operations, whether delivery is subcontracted or not. In cases where special loading, protection, or transportation techniques are involved, auditors will use the same criteria that apply to process control.

7.6   CONTROL OF MONITORING AND MEASURING DEVICES

The requirements in this section apply to monitoring and measuring devices (equipment) used for verifying product conformity. Strictly speaking, measuring devices used in production do not have to be included unless they are used for controlling processes (process control is in fact a form of in-process product verification). However, unless there are particular reasons to the contrary, all measuring devices should be controlled, regardless of whether they are used in inspection or production. In modern quality assurance systems, where production personnel are involved in inspections and products are verified indirectly through process control, there is no clear distinction between inspection and production functions.

In addition to conventional measuring instruments, the requirements of this section also apply to computer software used in automated inspection and testing equipment, and comparative test hardware such as jigs, templates, patterns, etc. For test hardware that cannot be calibrated, the term *calibration* should be interpreted to mean *checking accuracy*.

REQUIREMENT   ***Determine the requirements for the monitoring and measurement to be undertaken and select appropriate measuring devices that can meet these requirements.***

IMPLEMENTATION   The required tolerance of the measured value must be known. It should be specified in the technical documentation of the measured product, in inspection procedures, or by reference to relevant standards.

To ensure that the required accuracy will be attained, measuring devices should be selected on the basis of their capability, expressed in terms of accuracy, range, repeatability, and endurance under specified environmental conditions. Measurement uncertainty caused by differing environmental conditions and other factors, such as variation in the level of skill or method of operating the measuring device, should also be taken into account.

Formal repeatability and reproducibility (Gauge R&R) studies are not required in ISO 9001; however, there must be some knowledge of the gauge system total error, and defined criteria of acceptability. The criteria are usually expressed in terms of gauge system error as a percentage of specified part tolerance.

DOCUMENTATION The selection and use of measuring devices can be addressed in inspection procedures or in calibration procedures. In most situations, it is sufficient to include a general commitment to identify the required accuracy of measurements and to select appropriate measuring devices based on their documented capabilities. However, in situations where measurement accuracy is critical, fully developed procedures should be established (work instruction level). They should explain how to use measuring devices and how to determine the accuracy and uncertainty of a measurement.

RECORDS The records and evidence of compliance are documented criteria for selecting measuring devices, records of device accuracy checks, and, where applicable, measuring system analysis (Gauge R&R, stability, bias, linearity, etc.).

AUDIT Auditors will ask how the required accuracy of the measurements is known and documented, how the measurement system capability is determined, and how the influence of differing environmental conditions and other variation factors are accounted for.

REQUIREMENT

Calibrate or verify measuring devices at specified intervals, or prior to use, against international or national measurement standards.

IMPLEMENTATION

Standards used for calibration and checking of measuring devices must be certified and be traceable to an internationally or nationally recognized standard.

Every calibration should be evidenced by a calibration record, often called a calibration certificate. The certificate should:

- Identify the calibrated device by its name, type, and serial number;

- Identify the standard used for calibration and provide its traceability number to the national standard;

- List the calibrated modes or functions of the device and, where applicable, the accuracy attained;

- Identify the temperature, pressure, or other relevant environmental conditions; and

- Indicate the next calibration due date.

Companies that use an outside calibration service should require the service to provide such complete certificates. Calibration certificates do not necessarily need to be on paper. Electronic certificates are fully acceptable, as long as they contain all the required information and are properly secured.

Calibrated devices should be marked with calibration stickers indicating the last and the next calibration date. Measuring devices that are exempt from calibration must be clearly identified with warning labels, and should not be available in inspection areas.

DOCUMENTATION

The operational procedure for the control of measuring devices should define which types of devices must be calibrated, what restrictions govern the use of noncalibrated devices, who is responsible for the calibrating, the general policy regarding traceability of calibration standards, and the requirements for establishing and maintaining calibration records.

On the work instruction level, the calibration procedures should instruct how to calibrate and/or check specific types of devices, specify which calibration standards should be used, and provide forms or detailed instructions for establishing calibration certificates.

Instructions on how to calibrate specific types of devices may not be necessary when calibration instructions are provided in equipment manuals. If measuring devices are sent out for calibration to an outside calibration service, calibration instructions are not necessary.

RECORDS   The records and evidence of compliance consist of calibration procedures, certificates, and instructions, and the stickers identifying equipment calibration status.

AUDIT   To assess compliance, auditors will check the calibration status of devices found in production and inspections areas, and will ask for the corresponding calibration certificates. Auditors will also review a sample of the calibration instructions and may ask for checking and recalibration of some devices to verify that the devices were indeed accurately calibrated, and that the personnel performing calibrations know how to use the instructions. Reviewing calibration records, auditors will verify that traceability of standards (masters) used for calibration is documented, and may want to inspect the standards and their certificates.

REQUIREMENT   *Identify, control, safeguard and protect monitoring and measuring devices.*

IMPLEMENTATION   The backbone of any system for controlling the monitoring and measuring devices is an inventory and status list. Every device on the list is identified by its type and serial number, its usual location, the prescribed calibration periodicity, the last calibration date, and the next due date for calibration. The list is usually maintained on a computer. A standard database or a special software for management of calibration equipment can be used for this purpose.

Monitoring and measuring devices must be adequately maintained, protected, and stored. Devices should be stored in dedicated cabinets or drawers, and protective boxes should be used when provided. Defective or otherwise unsuitable devices should be segregated and/or identified with warning labels.

Measuring devices must be safeguarded against unauthorized adjustments that would invalidate the calibration setting. The most effective way is to seal the adjustment screws, or otherwise physically protect against tampering. If this is not possible or practical, there should be at least a clearly stated and communicated policy that unauthorized adjustments are prohibited. This policy can be displayed on warning labels or written in relevant procedures.

DOCUMENTATION The operational procedure for the control of measuring devices should explain how to establish and maintain the device inventory and status list; who is responsible for updating the list; what to do when a device cannot be located; and how to identify, maintain, store, and safeguard measuring devices.

RECORDS The records and evidence of compliance consist of the measuring device inventory and status list, calibration stickers, and the evidence that measuring devices are properly maintained and stored.

AUDIT Assessing compliance, auditors will check the actual status of measuring devices found in different areas against the device status list. They may also start from the other end: they will pick a couple of gauges from the list and check that the gauges can indeed be found in the designated areas and locations, and that the gauges are correctly identified with regard to their calibration status. Auditors will also verify that measuring devices are properly identified, maintained and stored, and that they are safeguarded against unauthorized adjustments.

REQUIREMENT

Reassess validity of previously made measurements when a nonconforming measuring device is discovered.

IMPLEMENTATION

When an out-of-calibration or otherwise nonconforming measuring device is discovered in the inspection or production areas, all measurements for which this device was used should be reassessed. In practice, this means that the affected products should be recalled to the inspection area and be verified again using approved and calibrated gauges. If the products have been already shipped, the customer should be notified.

The event of finding a nonconforming measuring device should be documented and brought to the attention of the responsible functions. Corrective actions should be implemented when appropriate.

DOCUMENTATION

The operational procedure for the control of monitoring and measuring devices should explain how to investigate suspect measurements and how to document these events, and should require that customers be notified when suspect products have been shipped. Investigation of causes and implementation of corrective actions should be also addressed in the procedure, or by reference to other procedures, for example, the corrective and preventive action procedure.

RECORDS

The records and evidence of compliance consist of nonconforming product reports, corrective action reports, internal audit reports, customer notifications, and other such documents established in the course of identifying and investigating the use of nonconforming measuring devices.

AUDIT

Auditors will ask whether there were instances of finding out-of-calibration gauges and will review documents and records pertaining to such events. Auditors will also review records of gauge condition and accuracy at the time when gauges are returned for calibration (if such records exist — they are not required in ISO 9001). If a precalibration record shows that a gauge was out of specified error limit, auditors will expect that the use of the gauge would have been investigated.

REQUIREMENT   *Validate, and periodically confirm, computer software used for verification of product conformity.*

IMPLEMENTATION   This requirement pertains specifically to inspection and testing equipment and systems that are controlled by custom software. Typical examples are equipment for testing electronic components, circuits, and media; automated optical or laser inspection systems; and test benches and simulators.

Although this requirement generally does not apply to software used for factory or process automation and control, it becomes relevant when process control is used to demonstrate product conformity, i.e., product is assumed to be conforming on the basis of process performance.

In practice, to satisfy this requirement there must be validation reports for custom software used in inspection or testing, which include software that is customized by the equipment manufacturer, or is developed in-house or by a consultant. These validation reports must clearly identify specific setups or modes that were validated, describe or reference methods used, and record the final results.

Software that was developed, installed, and used prior to the implementation of the quality system can be grandfathered in on the basis of its satisfactory performance, and does not have to be validated. But this needs to be formally justified and documented, to include precise identification of the software and its revision level, and the date when it was initially installed.

DOCUMENTATION   The operational procedure for the control of measuring devices should confirm the commitment to validate and control inspection and test software and should define the framework for these activities. In addition to defining requirements for validating in-house developed software, the procedure should require that vendors and consultants supplying or developing software be selected on the basis of their ability to validate the software, and that the requirements for the validation be included in purchase orders.

RECORDS

The records and evidence of compliance are software validation reports, or certificates grandfathering in software that was installed prior to the implementation of the quality system.

AUDIT

To assess compliance, auditors will ask for, and try to identify for themselves, where inspection and testing software is used, and will review the corresponding validation reports. They will verify that the software is identified and controlled with respect to its revision level and that the validation applies to the current revision. Auditors will also note whether the scope and modes of validation cover the setup in which the software is actually used.

MEASUREMENT, ANALYSIS AND IMPROVEMENT

8.1   GENERAL

REQUIREMENT

Define and implement monitoring and measurement needed to demonstrate conformity of product and the quality system, and to identify opportunities for improvement.

IMPLEMENTATION

This is yet another clause pertaining to quality planning. The overall approach to quality planning in ISO 9001:2000 is discussed under Clause 5.4.2.

The language in this clause is very general and it is difficult to identify particular requirements. It seems that the clause is calling for planning and implementation of the actual methods to be used for measuring product and process characteristics and quality system performance.

In practice, defining methods and equipment for measuring products and processes means specific instructions on how to make measurements, calculate results, and which equipment to use. For measuring quality system performance, it means instructions on what data and information to collect and how, and how to process and analyze the data.

DOCUMENTATION

The quality manual should include a general commitment to define and plan measurement and monitoring activities, and outline how this planning is developed and documented. This can be by reference to other clauses, such as 7.1, for example.

There is no need for a special operational procedure. Individual procedures and work instructions dealing with various activities that involve measuring and monitoring should define which methods and equipment to use, or who has the authority to make these decisions. The best system is to actually call out specific measuring equipment and/or test methods in quality plans for product realization and verification (refer to Clause 7.1). This would be especially relevant when product verification involves laboratory testing or analysis.

RECORDS Planning of measurement and monitoring activities would manifest itself in various documents defining the techniques, methods, and equipment to be used for these activities. The documentation may be in any form, such as specifications, procedures, work instructions, control plans, process sheets, etc.

AUDIT This clause is so vague and general that it is not readily auditable. If there are specific problems with planning of monitoring and measurement activities, auditors would rather use clauses 7.1, 8.2.3, or 8.2.4. This clause will only be invoked when the overall scope of monitoring and measuring is completely inadequate.

8.2 MONITORING AND MEASUREMENT

8.2.1 Customer Satisfaction

REQUIREMENT *Define and implement measures for obtaining and using information on customer satisfaction.*

IMPLEMENTATION In this clause the standard requires development of specific methods to obtain and evaluate information about customer satisfaction. The resulting data should be quantifiable, so that it can be used to determine the performance of the quality management system. For the purpose of this clause, *customer satisfaction* is defined as "customer perception as to whether the organization has fulfilled customer requirements."

The actual methods for measuring customer satisfaction would be very different from one industry to another, depending on the nature of the product, relationship with the customer, extent of the market, etc. Common methods include conducting customer satisfaction surveys, enclosing satisfaction rating cards with product, measuring frequency of repeat customers, categorizing customer complaints, and measuring rates of returned product.

DOCUMENTATION The quality manual should outline the processes and assign responsibilities for measuring customer satisfaction and for using this information.

While the standard does not explicitly require a written procedure, it requires that methods for obtaining and using the information shall be determined. As, in practice, *determined* means *documented*, there must be some type of documentation explaining what kind of information is to be gathered, and how; and how the information is to be processed, analyzed, and used. This might as well be a procedure.

When appropriate, in smaller organizations, this procedure could be merged with other procedures dealing with customer-related processes, such as determination of customer requirements (Clause 7.2.1), or customer communication and customer complaints (Clause 7.2.3).

The procedure should instruct how information about customer satisfaction and dissatisfaction is obtained, who is responsible for this activity, how the information is processed and communicated, and how it is used to improve the quality system.

RECORDS The records and evidence of compliance consist of data and information on customer satisfaction, and reports compiling and analyzing this information for presentation to the top executive management.

AUDIT Auditors will verify that methods for measuring customer satisfaction and dissatisfaction are determined (documented) and implemented, and provide consistent and meaningful data. Auditors will also focus on how the data is processed to provide quantifiable indicators and trends, and how it is used to improve the quality management system.

In practice, the most common problem is lack of consistency from one period to another, or against planned scope and methods. Many people also have a problem explaining how customer satisfaction data is used as a measurement of quality system performance.

8.2.2   Internal Audit

REQUIREMENT   *Plan internal audits, taking into consideration the importance and status of activities and results of previous audits.*

IMPLEMENTATION   All activities (processes) comprising the quality system should be audited at least once a year. Quality systems under implementation, and for the first year or two of operation, should be audited more frequently, every three or six months, for example. Even for mature systems, those activities that are especially important should be audited more frequently. The internal audit can be carried out all at once, as certification audits are, or can be distributed throughout the whole auditing cycle. The distributed way is preferable in most cases.

A popular format for an audit plan is a matrix with vertical listings of all quality system elements (activities) and horizontal listings of all departments and areas in the company. In the blocks where the elements and areas intersect, the planned audit dates can be written in or, if a given activity is not relevant in an area, the block can be crossed out. This format ensures that all quality system elements will be audited in all relevant areas, i.e., that nothing will be missed. Certification auditors use such matrices when planning their audits.

DOCUMENTATION   The operational procedure dealing with internal audits should explain what criteria need to be applied when planning internal audits, how to establish and document the audit plan, and who is responsible for establishing the plan and monitoring its execution.

RECORDS   There are no records of this activity, other than the internal audit plan itself.

AUDIT   To verify compliance, auditors will review the internal audit plan, noting if all relevant activities and areas are included, and if the frequency of auditing reflects the maturity of the quality system, the importance of individual activities, and results of previous audits. An audit plan where all activities are audited with the same frequency (once a year, for example) will automatically trigger a finding.

REQUIREMENT   *Define the internal audit process, criteria, scope, frequency, and methods.*

IMPLEMENTATION   The requirement here is for an operational procedure defining the internal audit process. The aspects that need to be defined are audit criteria, scope, frequency, and methods.

The audit criteria must include compliance of the quality system with ISO 9001, as well as the implementation and effectiveness of the system. The scope and frequency are usually determined and documented in the audit plan, as discussed in the preceding requirement. The methods would typically include preparation for the audit (checklists), initiation of the audit (opening meeting), and conducting the audit (objective evidence). Other relevant issues that are discussed in the next three requirements are auditor's qualifications and independence, implementation of corrective actions to address audit findings, and reporting the audit (findings).

Internal auditors should prepare for each audit. The preparation may include review of the ISO 9001 standard and procedures relevant to the audited activity. Quality records, including previous audit reports, corrective action requests, and product nonconformity reports should also be reviewed.

It is recommended that auditors use checklists. Preparing for the audit, auditors should develop their own checklists for the particular audit, or supplement standard checklists to include questions pertaining to systems, activities, and current projects that are unique to the company and the time of the audit. Using standard checklists without any customization is counterproductive. Auditors should focus on specific current and potential problems, rather than mechanically ticking off a standard checklist.

The audit is usually initiated with an opening meeting, where auditors explain the audit criteria, scope, and process to the departments or areas to be audited.

DOCUMENTATION The standard explicitly requires an operational procedure defining all aspects of the audit process. The procedure should cover the following issues:

- Internal audit planning and scheduling;
- Preparation for the audit and assignment of auditors;
- Rules and instructions for conducting the audit;
- Reporting of audit findings; and
- Corrective and preventive actions and closeout of findings.

RECORDS The records and evidence of compliance are audit plans, schedules, checklists, notes, reports, and corrective and preventive actions. There may also be some records of communication between auditors and managers of the audited departments.

AUDIT Auditors will carefully examine the internal audit procedure to assess whether it sufficiently defines the audit process, and will review records of selected audits to verify that the procedure was indeed followed. In this area auditors have a clear advantage because they know the subject so well. They will quickly get a feel for whether the internal audit system is effective or not. Common problems are the preparation for audit being too mechanical (standard checklist), and lack of consistency in approach and methods between different auditors.

REQUIREMENT   *Ensure that auditors are qualified, objective, and impartial, and shall not audit their own work.*

IMPLEMENTATION   Auditors must be independent from those responsible for the audited activity. Consequently, if the audits are usually conducted by the quality manager, someone else should be appointed to audit the quality assurance functions.

Qualifications of auditors should be evidenced by training records. These can be certificates from courses and seminars for auditors, or internal training provided by a consultant or someone in the company who is already qualified. Self-study training can also be accepted, but it must be formally recorded.

DOCUMENTATION   The procedure for internal auditing should clearly state the policy that auditors must be independent; specify qualification and training requirements for auditors; and instruct how to prepare for, and conduct, the audit.

RECORDS   The evidence of compliance consists of auditor training and qualification records, and audit checklists, if these are used and retained. Also, the audit reports will provide the evidence of auditor independence.

AUDIT   Assessing compliance, third-party auditors may want to interview some internal auditors, asking about how they learned to conduct audits and how they prepare for an audit. Reviewing internal audit reports, the auditors will also verify that the assigned internal auditors are independent of the audited activity.

REQUIREMENT   *Promptly implement actions to eliminate identified nonconformities and their causes.*

IMPLEMENTATION   Every nonconformity identified during an internal audit should automatically cause a request for corrective action. While in other situations the need for a corrective action can be evaluated and decided upon, there is no such freedom in the case of quality system audits. The quality system must comply with ISO 9001 at all times without exception.

For this reason, internal audits usually have their own integrated corrective action system. The same forms for reporting audit findings are also used for implementing corrective actions and for follow-up audits. But this integrated processing is the only difference. Otherwise, corrective actions resulting from internal audits must follow exactly the same rules that apply in general to corrective actions (see Clause 8.5.2).

DOCUMENTATION The operational procedure dealing with internal audits should clearly state the policy that all identified nonconformities must be followed up with corrective actions. The procedure should explain the process and responsibilities for requesting, implementing, and verifying corrective actions, or refer to another procedure that already explains the corrective action system (see Clause 8.5.2).

RECORDS The records and evidence of compliance are the internal audit reports, in particular sections for reporting on corrective actions and follow-up audits.

AUDIT Assessing compliance, auditors will review internal audit reports, noting if corrective actions are being implemented in a timely manner, and if all are followed up to verify their implementation and effectiveness.

REQUIREMENT *Record and report results of internal audits.*

IMPLEMENTATION A popular system for reporting internal audits is based on a one-page form for recording and processing each individual finding. The form is very similar to that used for processing and recording corrective actions. It has the following four blocks:

Heading: for recording the particulars of the audit, such as identification of the audited location and activity, name of the auditor and the manager responsible for the audited area, etc.;

Nonconformity: for describing the nonconforming condition and classification of the nonconformity;

Corrective Action: for describing the proposed action and the agreed implementation due date;

Follow up: for recording the result of the follow-up audit and closing the nonconformity.

Such a form is included in Jack Kanholm's *ISO 9000 Documentation* software.

When a finding is noted, the auditor fills out the *Heading* and the *Nonconformity* blocks, and then passes the form to the manager responsible for the audited area, who uses the third block, *Corrective Action,* to propose a corrective action. On or shortly after the implementation due date, the auditor comes back to the area to verify that the corrective action has been implemented and that it is effective. The result of the follow-up audit is recorded in the last block of the form, *Follow up*. The final report for the audit can be put together by adding a cover page to the individual pages reporting each nonconformity. The cover page would provide audit particulars (date of the audit, audited areas, names of auditors, etc.) and a brief summary of audit results.

At the end of the auditing cycle, when all activities and areas have been audited, the individual audit reports should be bound together and submitted for review to the executive management. This is normally done in conjunction with the scheduled management reviews of the quality system (see Clause 5.6). To facilitate the review, the final report should also contain statistics, conclusions, and recommendations.

DOCUMENTATION The operational procedure dealing with internal audits should explain how to use the audit nonconformity report forms, instruct how to prepare the final report for the whole audit cycle, assign the responsibility for preparing the report, and explain

how the report should be submitted and/or presented to the management review.

RECORDS   The records are, of course, the internal audit reports
themselves.

AUDIT   Assessing compliance, auditors will review the internal audit reports, noting if they are established,
processed, and evaluated by management in accordance with the governing procedures. A common
problem with nonconformity reports is that corrective
actions are not followed up in a timely manner.

8.2.3   Monitoring and Measurement of Processes

REQUIREMENT   *Monitor and measure quality system processes to demonstrate the ability of the system to achieve planned results.*

IMPLEMENTATION   This clause is somewhat redundant, but it introduces
a new principle: that the performance of the quality
system should be monitored and measured to verify
its ability to achieve planned objectives. In practice,
this means setting specific, measurable objectives,
and checking whether these objectives are being
achieved within specified time frames.

There is no need to establish new systems or processes to implement this requirement. There are already
several systems required elsewhere in the standard
that can be employed for setting objectives, for monitoring and measuring the system, and for initiating
corrective and preventive actions to address deficiencies. For example, objectives can be set within
the framework of quality objectives (5.4.1) and management reviews (5.6); while monitoring and measurement may be based on internal audits (8.2.2),
customer satisfaction (8.2.1), analysis of data (8.4),
nonconforming product (8.3), or subcontractor performance (7.4.1). Identified deficiencies may be
addressed using the corrective and preventive action

systems (8.5.2 and 8.5.3), or through the continual improvement program (8.5.1).

DOCUMENTATION The quality manual should clearly state the commitment to monitor and measure the performance of the quality system, and identify those activities that will be used for setting objectives, monitoring and measuring performance, and initiating actions to correct deficiencies. There is usually no need for a dedicated operational procedure to address this requirement, but the manual should reference all procedures pertaining to the related activities.

RECORDS The primary records and evidence of compliance are internal audit reports, management review minutes, and corrective and preventive action reports.

AUDIT Auditors will look for evidence that performance and status of the quality system are determined and reported (internal audits, quality performance data, etc.), and that these results are compared against quality objectives and other planned results. There should also be evidence that when planned results are not achieved, corrective action is taken. Much of this evidence will be found in management review records.

8.2.4   Monitoring and Measurement of Product

REQUIREMENT *Verify that product requirements have been met at appropriate stages of production and/or service provision.*

IMPLEMENTATION This is usually referred to as in-process inspection and testing, and include all verification activities between the acceptance of incoming materials and submission of the product for final inspection and testing. In-process inspections are not mandatory in all cases. To determine at which stages of production in-process inspections should be conducted, the following questions should be answered:

■ Can all the critical characteristics and aspects of a product be inspected at final inspection? If the answer is "Yes," in-process inspections are not mandatory. If the answer is "No," the next question is:

- Is the process responsible for the characteristic a special process, i.e., is validated and formally controlled in accordance with Clause 7.5.2? If the answer is "Yes," the in-process inspection is not mandatory.

In other words, in-process inspections are only mandatory for those processes that are not validated and whose results are covered up by subsequent processing before the product is finished. While these are the minimum requirements, most companies will have a much more extensive in-process inspection program to avoid further processing of a nonconforming product.

In-process inspections can be carried out by production personnel as self-inspections. But the system must be just as formal and in compliance with the relevant ISO 9001 requirements as if the inspection function was independent. Self-inspections should be identified and carried out as distinct operations.

All in-process inspections must be specified in control plans or other documents resulting from quality planning (Clause 7.1). Where production work orders or travellers are used, the inspections can be called out as distinct operations. At the points where in-process inspections are called out, products should be held and identified to prevent them from moving on to the next processing stage before they are inspected. Suitable arrangements should be provided for this purpose. Products that fail an in-process inspection should be labeled and segregated.

DOCUMENTATION   An operational procedure for in-process inspections is normally not necessary, as all relevant issues would have been already addressed in other procedures and work instructions. These issues are planning and defining the program of in-process inspections for a product, responsibilities for conducting the inspections, identification of inspection status, segregation of nonconforming product, and establishment of inspection records. However, despite the redundancy, many companies may want to have such a procedure anyway, especially as it was required in the previous edition of the standard. Work instructions for carrying out specific inspections and tests may be also necessary, depending on the nature and complexity of these activities.

RECORDS The records and evidence of compliance consist of in-process inspection records and implemented measures for holding products until they pass inspection (inspection status identification). Inspection records will be discussed in more detail at the end of this section.

AUDIT Assessing compliance, auditors will review in-process inspection records and will verify that adequate measures are employed to prevent uninspected or nonconforming products from being passed to the next processing stage. As with all types of inspections, auditors will also examine inspector qualification records, measuring and test equipment, and inspection procedures.

REQUIREMENT *Do not proceed with product release and/or service delivery until conformity of product has been verified.*

IMPLEMENTATION This is usually referred to as final inspection. It consists of checking that all required receiving and in-process inspections have been carried out with satisfactory results, and completing the physical inspections and tests that are still needed to fully verify that the product meets the specified requirements.

Inspectors responsible for the final inspection should review quality records established at preceding stages, checking that all operations are completed; that all inspections prescribed by the quality plans were carried out; and, if applicable, that the traceability record is complete. Then inspectors should carry out the remaining inspections, establish records of these inspections, and release the product.

Product release must be recorded and include the identity of the person authorizing the release. This is usually done by signing or stamping appropriate documents and marking or labeling the released products.

DOCUMENTATION   Although an operational procedure for final inspection is not required, many companies would want to have such a procedure to make sure that inspectors are well instructed about accepting and releasing products. The procedure should explain the two-stage nature of the inspection (i.e., review of preceding inspection records and completion of physical inspections); assign the responsibility for carrying out the inspections; instruct how to identify and segregate conforming and nonconforming products; and explain what needs to be done to formally release products to stock or shipping. There should also be specific inspection instructions providing checklists for documents (quality records) that must be reviewed, and product characteristics and modes of operations that must be inspected and tested.

RECORDS   The evidence of compliance consists of final inspection records and markings or labels evidencing the acceptance and release of product. Records will be discussed in more detail in the next section.

AUDIT   Auditors will review the final inspections records and will examine the methods used for releasing products. As with other types of inspections, auditors will also examine inspector qualification records, the inspection equipment, and the final inspection and testing instructions. Except for the most simple and obvious cases, the instructions should provide checklists for the review of quality records and for the physical inspections and tests.

REQUIREMENT   *Maintain records with evidence of product conformity and identity of the person authorizing the release of product.*

IMPLEMENTATION   In most cases an inspection record does not need to be more elaborate than a sign-off or a stamp on an inspection card or other document associated with the inspected product. For example, the receiving inspection can be recorded by signing off the receiving copy of a purchase order, while the in-process and final inspections can be recorded by signing off the work order where the inspections are called out. Other commonly used methods for establishing inspection records are marking up and signing a copy of a drawing, filling out and signing inspection forms, issuing testing reports, and so forth.

There must also be a record of product release, to include identification of the person authorizing the release. This is usually combined with the final inspection record.

DOCUMENTATION Instructions for establishing inspection records should be documented. It can be done on two levels. An operational procedure should provide general requirements, assign responsibilities, and deal with distribution and filing; and specific inspection procedures (work instructions) should provide forms or detailed instructions for recording specific types of inspections. For simple inspections, or when special forms are not used, the whole system can be explained solely in the operational procedure.

RECORDS The records and evidence of compliance are the inspection records themselves.

AUDIT Reviewing inspection and testing records, auditors will verify that the records are properly established, that they are legible and in good condition, that they are retained for a specified period of time, and that they are properly organized and readily retrievable. For product release records, auditors will note whether the identity of the person releasing product is identified.

A frequent problem is a failure to completely fill out in all relevant fields on inspection forms, and forms that suggest an inspection scope that is greater than the one actually carried out. If a form is outdated, it should be modified. If a field does not apply, it should be crossed out or be marked with NA (Not Applicable). When a field is blank, auditors assume that relevant information was left out.

8.3   CONTROL OF NONCONFORMING PRODUCT

REQUIREMENT   *Identify and control nonconforming product and maintain records of nonconformities and actions taken.*

IMPLEMENTATION   Product is considered nonconforming when it is in any way different from the specified product and/or approved sample. Nonconformity can be a characteristic that is out of tolerance; a workmanship problem; differing color, texture, or surface finish; an appearance defect; damage resulting from improper handling or storage; and so forth.

Product nonconformities are usually detected at various inspection and testing points. They may also be found by customers, and the products are returned for rework or replacement. As soon as a nonconformity is detected, the nonconforming product should be identified — with a red HOLD, NONCONFORMITY, or REJECTED label, for example — and be segregated, or even quarantined, whenever possible.

The nature of the nonconformity must be documented (recorded). This is usually done in a nonconformity report form. The same form can also be used to record the disposition and, when relevant, reinspection of repaired or reworked products. The form can have the following four sections:

Heading: for identifying the products and the location where they were found.

Description of Nonconformity: for documenting the nature of the nonconformity.

Disposition: for recording the decision regarding what should be done with the nonconforming product.

Close-out: for recording acceptance of the product after rework or repair.

Such a form is provided and explained in Jack Kanholm's *ISO 9000 Documentation* software.

Copies of nonconformity reports should be distributed to functions concerned, for example, sales, purchasing, production control, and quality assurance.

DOCUMENTATION ISO 9001 explicitly requires a written operational procedure for controlling nonconforming products. The procedure should explain how nonconforming products are identified and segregated; how nonconformities are recorded; and how nonconformities are reported to other functions concerned, including those responsible for making disposition decisions.

RECORDS The records consist of reports documenting product nonconformities and disposition decisions. The use of labels, tags, and other means to identify nonconforming products, and their segregation, provide additional evidence of implementation.

AUDIT Assessing compliance, auditors will verify that all nonconforming products, wherever they are found, are clearly identified and segregated. Auditors will also review nonconformity reports, noting if the reports are used consistently every time a nonconformity is identified, and if they are further processed and distributed to document the disposition decisions and inform other functions concerned.

REQUIREMENT *Take appropriate action to deal with nonconforming product.*

IMPLEMENTATION The standard defines three generic ways to deal with a nonconforming product:

- Eliminate nonconformity: reprocess or rework product to fully meet specified requirements. After the product is reworked or reprocessed, it must be verified (reinspected) to confirm that it now meets requirements.

- Accept-as-is: authorize product use, release or acceptance. This decision can only be made by explicitly authorized engineers, managers, or supervisors, and, where applicable, must be agreed to by the customer. This is often referred to as acceptance under concession.

- Scrap or regrade: preclude the original intended use or application. Scrapped and regraded product must be appropriately identified and segregated.

Although not mentioned in the standard, in many industries there is also an option to repair a nonconforming product to meet at least the most critical requirements, without being able to restore full conformity. This case is a hybrid of the first and second options: elimination of the nonconformity is only partial, and thus the product must be accepted as-is by concession.

The authority for the disposition of nonconforming product must be defined in a procedure. The authority can be assigned on different levels depending on the nature of the nonconformity and the product, and the disposition decision itself. For example, decisions to rework or scrap can usually be made by supervisors or even production personnel, while accept-as-is and repair decisions may require involvement of higher authority.

The disposition decision must be documented and authorized with a signature. It is best to do it in the same nonconformity report that is opened when a nonconforming product is first identified. With accept-as-is, regrade, and scrap decisions, the nonconformity report can be closed out right away. When the decision is to rework or repair, closing out the report must wait until the products are reinspected.

Control should be established over the disposal of nonconforming material that is designated as scrap, to ensure clear identification so that the nonconforming material cannot be mixed up with conforming product or re-enter the production system. Safe disposal measures should also be established, if applicable.

DOCUMENTATION The operational procedure dealing with the disposition of nonconforming products should define the possible disposition decisions, and provide guidelines and assign the authority for making the decisions. The procedure should also explain how to use the nonconformity reports for recording nonconforming product dispositions.

RECORDS

The records and the evidence of compliance are the nonconformity reports that document disposition decisions, and records demonstrating that repaired and reworked products are reinspected.

AUDIT

Auditors will review nonconformity reports, noting if dispositions are being authorized at the appropriate level. They will also verify that accepted nonconformities are recorded to denote the actual condition and that repaired and reworked products are reinspected.

REQUIREMENT

When nonconforming product is detected after delivery, take action to mitigate the effects of the nonconformity.

IMPLEMENTATION

To people in regulated industries, such as medical devices, automotive, drugs, or food, this will immediately sound like a requirement for a product recall procedure. And this is exactly how this requirement should be interpreted in cases where product nonconformity may create public safety hazard. In other industries it may be sufficient to express a general commitment to take appropriate actions without the need for a formal recall procedures.

DOCUMENTATION

Whether public safety is an issue or not, the quality manual should at least state the commitment to undertake appropriate actions to mitigate the effects of a nonconforming delivery. The existing systems for processing customer complaints and/or for initiating corrective and preventive actions may be used for documenting, initiating, and monitoring these actions.

In addition, where public safety is a potential issue, auditors will expect a procedure for conducting a recall of defective products, and/or for advising customers how to handle such products (advisory notices).

RECORDS

As no systems or procedures are explicitly required, the evidence of compliance will consist of records demonstrating that mitigating actions were indeed taken where appropriate.

AUDIT　　Auditors will actively seek to identify historical cases of nonconforming deliveries from records (customer complaints) and interviews, and will follow up to determine what specific actions were taken in particular cases. Where public safety is a potential issue, auditors will expect more formalized recall procedures and records.

8.4　　ANALYSIS OF DATA

REQUIREMENT　　*Collect and analyze quality performance data to demonstrate the effectiveness of the quality system and to identify opportunities for improvement.*

IMPLEMENTATION　　The standard lists four categories of data and information that must be collected and analyzed: customer satisfaction, conformity to product requirements, characteristics of processes and products, and supplier performance.

Although this is an independent requirement and has to be acknowledged on a general level, the actual activities that include collecting of the required data would be developed in response to other clauses of the standard. For example, collecting data regarding product conformity would result from activities required in Clauses 8.2.4 and 8.3; and customer satisfaction data would result from implementation of Clause 8.2.1.

Most organizations already collect and track quality-related data, such as reject rates, late deliveries, or various productivity indicators. To comply with ISO 9001 these systems need to be expanded to include all four categories of data required in this clause, and they need to be formally documented.

DOCUMENTATION　　The quality manual should identify activities that involve collection of quality-related data; assign appropriate responsibilities; and determine how the data should be communicated, analyzed and used to identify opportunities for improvement.

A documented procedure is not explicitly required, however, a procedure for coordinating the gathering and processing of quality performance data would be quite useful in many organizations, as this is a collaborative process involving may departments and functions. Without a procedure it will be difficult to assure continuity and consistency of these activities throughout the organization.

If established, the procedure should define the nature and scope of collected data, prescribe specific methods and frequencies, determine formats, assign responsibilities, and instruct how the data should be communicated and to whom. The procedure should instruct how the data should be processed and analyzed, and how it is to be used by the management to identify opportunities for improvement (usually through the management review process).

RECORDS

Records and evidence of compliance are the actual raw data collected, and reports with the analysis and conclusions. Management review records may also be relevant to demonstrate that the information is used to identify improvement opportunities.

AUDIT

Auditors will verify that all required data are collected systematically and consistently. Consistency is the key word. The most common problem is lack of continuity and consistency in those categories where there may be inadequate resources committed to collect and analyze the data. Auditors will also verify that this information is actually used for identifying improvement opportunities (usually by examining management review records).

8.5   IMPROVEMENT

8.5.1   Continual Improvement

REQUIREMENT *Continually improve the effectiveness of the quality management system.*

IMPLEMENTATION In ISO 9001:2000 continual improvement is not a discreet process or element of the quality system, but rather a way of managing the system. The thinking goes like this: The quality system has processes for establishing quality objectives, for implementing operational controls to achieve the objectives, and for measuring the results. If the results fail to meet the objectives, it is the fault of the quality system. The system must be improved so that it becomes more effective in reaching the objectives. When the objectives are achieved, new objectives are set and the quality system is improved again to meet the new challenges.

In a nutshell, this clause requires that opportunities and priorities for improvement of the quality system be identified by comparing the actual quality performance to objectives defined in the quality policy and quality objectives. The actual quality performance is determined by analyzing customer satisfaction information, product and process conformity data, supplier performance data, internal audit results, and other data and information relevant to quality performance. Management review considers all relevant information and defines priorities for improving the quality system. Corrective and preventive actions and special management programs are the means for implementing improvements. In this model there are no new elements or activities. All necessary quality system processes are already required elsewhere in the standard. This clause only instructs how to use the system to facilitate improvement.

The most common approach is to implement continual improvement within the framework of management reviews. Clause 5.6.3 already requires that every management review be concluded with actions related to improvement of the quality system and products.

This clause does not require planning and establishment of specific management programs for achieving continual improvement actions or objectives. In fact, it does not even ask for any actions or objectives (although Clause 5.6.3 does). It only requires that the effectiveness of the quality system be continually improved. However, in real life, management decisions regarding continual improvement must be expressed as specific actions, and there must be a system for monitoring implementation of these actions. Otherwise nothing will be done. Auditors know this, and may want to verify that improvement-related actions are being consistently implemented.

DOCUMENTATION The procedure for continual improvement is often documented as a section within the management review procedure. However, to emphasize their commitment to the continual improvement philosophy, some companies may want to have it as a separate document. The procedure should explain how the quality policy, objectives, internal audit results, analysis of data, corrective and preventive action, and management review are used to facilitate continual improvement.

RECORDS To demonstrate compliance, the management review records should include evidence that all relevant issues and information were presented and discussed, and the review output should include actions related to improvement of the quality system (the same is required in Clause 5.6.3).

AUDIT Auditing continual improvement is quite difficult, because the requirements are so vague and because so many other elements (processes) of the quality system are involved. Auditors will know what to look for, but will have a difficult time finding solid objective evidence to support their conclusions.

The obvious way out is to audit against whatever the auditee's documentation commits them to do. But if the documentation is just as vague and general as the standard, this approach will not work. The only solid ground is in Clause 5.4.1, Quality Objectives, requiring that specific, measurable (improvement) objectives be established; and in Clause 5.6.3, Management Review Output, asking for management reviews to be concluded with actions to improve the quality system.

8.5.2   Corrective Action

REQUIREMENT   *Investigate causes of nonconformities, take corrective actions to prevent recurrence, and review the effectiveness of actions taken.*

IMPLEMENTATION   The system for investigating quality problems and implementing corrective actions should include the following elements:

- Identification and description of the nonconforming condition;

- Decision about whether a request for corrective action is the appropriate response and if any action will be requested;

- Formal request for corrective action;

- Proposal of a plan for corrective action and a deadline for its implementation; and

- Verification that the corrective action has been implemented and that it is effective.

The authority for deciding whether a corrective action will be requested is usually placed relatively high in the organization, especially when implementation of the action is likely to cause disruption and require considerable resources.

Corrective action requests should be addressed directly to the department or function that is responsible for the nonconforming condition and is capable of correcting it. The responsible party should acknowledge that the description of the nonconforming condition is accurate, and should propose, in writing, the action to be taken and the estimated date of completion. The requesting party should then review and approve the proposed action, and, on or immediately after the agreed completion date, should follow up to verify that the action has been implemented and that it is effective. The whole process can be documented using a corrective action request form, containing separate

148   ISO 9001 REQUIREMENTS

blocks for description of the nonconforming condition, proposal of the corrective action to be taken, and follow-up verification. An example of this type of a form is included in Jack Kanholm's *ISO 9001 Documentation* software.

At the beginning of this section, it was mentioned that the need for implementing a corrective action can be identified by different functions and/or departments within the company. Typically, these are quality assurance/control, customer service, process control, purchasing, and internal quality auditing. One possibility is to allow each such function to have its own independent system for requesting and implementing corrective actions. Another possibility is to have a central system through which all requests for corrective actions must be processed, regardless of where and how they originate.

DOCUMENTATION The standard explicitly requires a written operational procedure dealing with corrective actions. It should clearly define functions vested with the authority to request corrective actions, explain the process, and instruct how to use the corrective action request forms. When different functions and/or departments operate their own systems, each should have their own procedure.

RECORDS The records and evidence of compliance are the corrective action requests. Open requests under processing should be appropriately organized and/or logged to ensure that they will be followed up when due. Closed-out requests should be filed and retained for a specified period of time.

When returned products are involved, the records of corrective actions should include the description of the product and the code number, including the product batch numbers or serial numbers when applicable; description of the quality problem; records of investigation of the underlying causes; the action to be taken; and evidence that the corrective action was implemented and that it is effective.

AUDIT

When assessing compliance, auditors will review the corrective action requests, noting whether the requests are processed in a timely manner and are properly closed out, i.e., are signed off after the verification of their implementation and effectiveness. Auditors will also ask for a log or a listing of customer returns and will investigate specific cases to verify whether returned products are being consistently investigated.

8.5.3   Preventive Action

REQUIREMENT

Identify potential nonconformities and their causes and take actions to prevent their occurrence.

IMPLEMENTATION

The distinction between corrective and preventive action is that corrective action deals with actual nonconformities and preventive action deals with potential nonconformities. The only difference in processing of corrective and preventive action is the first step of identifying the problem that requires attention. All other steps of the process can be exactly the same for both, and there is usually no need to have independent systems and procedures.

The usual sources of information needed to identify potential quality problems are process performance data, product nonconformity reports, manufacturing equipment maintenance records, customer complaints, product servicing records, and other such quality records. Most of the recorded problems are usually minor and, when looked at individually, may not warrant initiation of corrective actions. But when analyzed over time, the records may show decreasing quality capability or other unfavorable trends that must be dealt with to reduce the probability that a nonconformity will occur.

DOCUMENTATION

Although the standard explicitly requires a written operational procedure dealing with preventive actions, it does not mean that it must be an independent and dedicated procedure. The corrective and preventive action systems can be documented together, or preventive actions can be included in the procedure dealing with continual improvement. The procedure should assign the responsibility for analyzing quality records, and explain how the results of the analysis should be reported and used for initiating preventive actions. After the methods for identifying the need for a preventive action are defined, the rest of the procedure, i.e., the sections dealing with requesting and processing of the action, may be identical for both the preventive and corrective actions.

RECORDS

The records and evidence of compliance are reports and records from reviews of trends in quality performance data, and the preventive action requests.

AUDIT

Assessing compliance, auditors will review the preventive action requests, and will ask for the evidence that quality records and process performance data are being regularly reviewed and analyzed to determine where preventive actions may be required. The most common problem is that companies do not have any preventive actions to show, because they really do not distinguish between corrective and preventive actions, and process everything as corrective actions. Auditors take it as a sign that the system for preventive actions is not implemented; this could be a serious finding. Companies should make a conscious effort to specifically identify preventive actions.

APPENDIX

The following matrix attempts to establish correspondence between ISO 9001:1994 and ISO 9001:2000. This can only be done approximately, as the standard has been completely rewritten and reorganized. Many old elements from the 1994 edition are now scattered all around the standard, while others are completely taken out without a trace. There are also new elements in the 2000 edition that cannot be associated with any of the old clauses.

But this matrix, imperfect as it is, provides a quick overview of what has changed, and helps to understand the new requirements in the framework of the familiar 20 sections of the old 1994 edition.

ISO 9001:1994	ISO 9001:2000 and New Req.
4.1 Management responsibility	
4.1.1 Quality policy	5.1 + 5.3 + 5.4.1 New requirements: 1) 5.3 requires that the quality policy must include commitments to meeting requirements and to continual improvement; must provide framework for quality objectives; and must be periodically reviewed for continuing suitability; 2) 5.4.1 requires that measurable quality objectives must be established at all relevant functions and levels within the organization.
4.1.2 Organization	
4.1.2.1 Responsibility and authority	5.5.2 No new requirements The old requirement for organizational independence (freedom) is dropped.
4.1.2.2 Resources	5.1 + 5.6.3 + 6.1 + 6.3 No new requirements Although resources are addressed in several clauses, there are no new auditable requirements as such. The most specific is Clause 5.6.3, requiring designation of specific resources for improvement projects (actions).
4.1.2.3 Management representative	5.5.3 New requirement: 1) Management representative must promote awareness of customer requirements.

ISO 9001:1994	ISO 9001:2000 and New Req.
4.1.3 Management review	5.6 New requirements: 1) Management reviews must include review inputs and outputs, as listed in this clause; 2) Management reviews shall include actions related to improvement of the quality system and products.
4.2 Quality system	
4.2.1 General	4.1 + 4.2 + 4.2.2 New requirement: 1) 4.2.2 requires that any exclusions of ISO 9001 requirements must be identified and justified in the quality manual.
4.2.2 Quality system procedures	4.2 New requirement: 1) The quality system documentation must be sufficient to ensure effective operation and control of the system. (This will allow auditors to request additional documentation when there is evidence of system inefficiency.)
4.2.3 Quality Planning	5.4.2 + 7.1 + 8.1 New requirement: 1) Organizations must plan the quality management system and how to achieve quality objectives (5.4.2), and plan measuring and monitoring activities (8.1) The requirements for planning product realization processes and product validation activities are basically unchanged, but are defined in much more detail (Clause 7.1).
4.3 Contract Review	7.2.1 + 7.2.2 New requirement: 1) 7.2.1:requires that organizations must determine product requirements, to include those that are not specified but are necessary for use or compliance with laws and regulations.
4.4 Design Control	7.3 No new requirements Although some subclauses are completely rewritten, there are practically no new requirements.
4.5 Document and data control	4.2.3 No new requirements
4.6 Purchasing	7.4 New requirement: 1) There must be established criteria for evaluation and selection of suppliers, and for their periodic re-evaluations.

ISO 9001:1994	ISO 9001:2000 and New Req.
4.7 Control of customer-supplied product	7.5.4 No new requirements While the requirements are the same, the clause applies now to all customer property, including intellectual property (information).
4.8 Product identification & traceability	7.5.3 No new requirements
4.9 Process Control	6.3 + 6.4 + 7.1 + 7.5.1 + 7.5.2 New requirement: 1) Validation of special processes is now explicitly required. Otherwise no changes, although process control-related requirements are completely rewritten.
4.10 Inspection and testing	7.1 + 7.4.3 + 8.1 + 8.2.4 No new requirements There are important changes in vocabulary, approach, and organization of inspection and testing requirements, but the substance is basically unchanged.
4.11 Control of inspection, measuring and test equipment	7.6 No new requirements Note that validation of software used for product verification is now required much more explicitly.
4.12 Inspection and test status	7.5.3 No new requirements
4.13 Control of nonconforming product	8.3 New requirement: 1) When a nonconforming product is delivered, appropriate action must be taken to mitigate potential effects of the nonconformity.
4.14 Corrective and preventive action	8.5.2 + 8.5.3 No new requirements
4.15 Handling, storage, packaging, preservation and delivery	7.5.5 No new requirements This clause is cut back to a single, general statement and stripped of all specific requirements. However, it generally represents the same requirements as applied under ISO 9001:1994.
4.16 Control of quality records	4.2.4 No new requirements
4.17 Internal quality audits	8.2.2 No new requirements

ISO 9001:1994	ISO 9001:2000 and New Req.
4.18 Training	6.2.1 + 6.2.2 New requirements: 1) Organizations must evaluate the effectiveness of training provided; and 2) Employees must be aware of the importance of their activities and how they contribute to the achievement of quality objectives.
4.19 Servicing	Servicing now falls under the definition of *product*. Consequently, all requirements of the standard apply to servicing in the same way as they apply to other types of products.
4.20 Statistical Techniques	8.1 + 8.2.3 + 8.2.4 + 8.4 No new requirements There are actually no clauses dedicated to statistical techniques. The clauses listed above refer to activities where the use of statistical techniques could be relevant.
Customer satisfaction (no assignable clause)	5.2 + 7.2.1 + 7.2.3 + 8.2.1 New requirements: 1) 7.2.1:requires that organizations must determine product (customer) requirements (refer to ISO 9001:1994 Clause 4.3, Contract review); 2) 7.2.3 requires organizations to define and implement arrangements for communicating with customers; 3) 8.2.1 requires that organizations obtain and use information on customer satisfaction and dissatisfaction.
Continual improvement (no assignable clause)	5.4.1 + 5.6.2 + 5.6.3 + 8.4 + 8.5.1 New requirements: 1) 8.4 requires collecting and analyzing data to determine the effectiveness of the quality system and for identifying where improvements can be made; 2) 8.5.1 requires planning and management for continual improvement of the quality system, including the use of quality policy and objectives and quality performance data. New requirements in 5.4.1 and 5.6 were already identified under ISO 9001:1994 Clauses 4.1.1, Quality policy, and 4.1.3, Management review.

ISO 9000 by Jack Kanholm

ISO 9000 QUALITY MANUAL AND PROCEDURES

Fourth Edition

Computer software with quality manual, procedures and forms - $ 390.

Download Demo
at www.aqapress.com

This software is a unique resource for documenting ISO 9001:2000 system and upgrading from 1994 edition. It offers:

- A quality system that is simple, natural and free from excessive paperwork, and satisfies certification requirements.
- Fully developed two-level documentation, including quality manual, operational procedures and forms.

- Wizards and step-by-step tutorials for upgrading your old (1994) documentation.Thousands of companies have been successfully certified using this documentation (first published in 1992).

ISO 9000 REQUIREMENTS

92 Requirements Checklist and Compliance Guide

Fourth Edition

154 Pages
Hardcover Book - $ 39.

This book identifies 92 distinct, auditable requirements in ISO 9001:2000. Each requirement is explained with regard to interpretation, procedures, records, and relevant auditing practices. In essence, the book reinterprets the standard into a list of 92 specific actions that need to be taken to achieve compliance, and explains how to implement them in the organization.

Now in its fourth edition, and with over 40,000 copies sold, this book is established as the reference of choice for understanding and interpreting the ISO 9000 standards.

This is a general orientation course for ISO 9000.The workbook is intended for distribution to all personnel for self-study or group training. The course explains what the ISO 9000 standards are, how the quality system works, and how everyone should prepare themselves and their work areas for the certification audit. This course satisfies ISO 9000 requirements for training personnel in the quality system. It includes a short test and a certificate of completion.

ISO 9000 IN OUR COMPANY

Self-Study Course for Personnel

Fourth Edition

24 Pages Booklet - $ 9.

SATISFIED CUSTOMERS This ISO 9000 series was initially published in 1992 — the first in the USA. Over 32,000 companies have purchase these materials and some 80% have ordered additional copies or recommended the books to others. The lasting popularity of these materials is their best recommendation.

ISO 14000 by Jack Kanholm

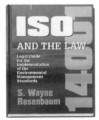

ISO 13485 & EN 46000

by Lynette Howard and Jack Kanholm

Download Demo

ISO 13485 (EN 46000) QUALITY SYSTEM MANUAL AND PROCEDURES

Computer software with quality manual, procedures and forms - $ 390.

ISO 13485 (EN 46000) REQUIREMENTS

99 Requirements Checklist and Compliance Guide

170 Pages
Hardcover Book - $ 59.

ISO 13485 (EN 46000) IN OUR COMPANY

Self-Study Course for Personnel

32-Page Booklet, Test and Certificate - $ 9.

QUALITY SYSTEM FOR THE MEDICAL DEVICE INDUSTRY

The three publications in this series provide: ready-made template documentation with the quality manual and operational procedures, explanation of all ISO 13485 and EN 46000 requirements, and a general orientation course for personnel. All three publications are based on Jack Kanholm's ISO 9000 series (refer to the preceding page annotating the ISO 9000 publications).

Ms. Howard contributed her unique knowledge of both the U.S. and European regulatory requirements.

QS-9000 & TS 16949

by Jack Kanholm   (for TS check our internet site)

Download Demo

QS-9000 QUALITY SYSTEM MANUAL AND PROCEDURES

Computer software with quality manual, procedures and forms - $ 390.

QS-9000 REQUIREMENTS

107 Requirements Checklist and Compliance Guide

177 Pages
Hardcover Book - $ 59.

QS-9000 IN OUR COMPANY

Self-Study Course for Personnel

32-Page Booklet, Test and Certificate - $ 9.

QUALITY SYSTEM FOR THE AUTOMOTIVE INDUSTRY

The three publications in this series provide: ready-made template documentation with the quality manual and operational procedures, explanation of all QS-9000 requirements, and a QS-9000 general orientation course for personnel. All three publications are based on Jack Kanholm's ISO 9000 series (refer to the preceding page annotating the ISO 9000 publications).

Since 1995 thousands of companies have used these materials to successfully achieve QS-9000 certification.

ORDER FORM

Qty	Title	Prc	Dsc	Total	Qty	Title	Prc	Dsc	Total
	ISO 9000:2000					**ISO 14000**			
	ISO 9000 Requirements	$ 39.	%			ISO 14001 Requirements	$ 49.	%	
	ISO 9000 In Our Company	$ 9.	%			ISO 14001 And The Law	$ 59.	%	
	ISO 9001 Standard	$ 48.	%			ISO 14001 In Our Company	$ 9.	%	
	ISO 9000 Template Manual and Procedures Software	$ 390.	%			ISO 14001 Template Manual and Procedures Software	$ 390.	%	
	QS-9000					**ISO 13485 (EN 46000)**			
	QS-9000 Requirements	$ 59.	%			ISO 13485 Requirements	$ 59.	%	
	QS-9000 In Our Company	$ 9.	%			ISO 13485 In Our Company	$ 9.	%	
	QS-9000 Template Manual and Procedures Software	$ 390.	%			ISO 13485 Template Manual and Procedures Software	$ 390.	%	

Sales tax of 7.75% (CA only) and shipping cost (see chart below) will be added to invoice

Quantity Discounts (copies per title)	Shipping (by UPS)
5 to 9: 10% 20 to 39: 30% Over 100: 50% 10 to 19: 20% 40 to 99: 40%	☐ Ground $ 6. ☐ 2nd Day $ 14. ☐ 3rd Day $ 9. ☐ Next Day $ 28.

Shipping Address (No PO Boxes)

Mr. ☐   Ms. ☐ _____

Title: _____

Company: _____

Street: _____

City: _____ State: _____ Zip: _____

Phone & Fax: _____

Billing Address

Company: _____

Street: _____

City: _____ State: _____ Zip: _____

Attention: _____

Method of Payment

Card No.: |___|___|___|___|___|___|___|___|___|___|___|___|___|

☐ Check   ☐ Visa   ☐ MC   ☐ AmEx   Exp.: _____

☐ Bill Company Purchase Order No.: _____

Signature & Date: _____

ISO 9000 REQUIREMENTS

To order, fax this form to (626) 796 9070 or call (800) 600 3601